Get the eBook FREE!

(PDF, ePub, Kindle, and liveBook all included)

We believe that once you buy a book from us, you should be able to read it in any format we have available. To get electronic versions of this book at no additional cost to you, purchase and then register this book at the Manning website.

Go to https://www.manning.com/freebook and follow the instructions to complete your pBook registration.

That's it!
Thanks from Manning!

T0076342

Regular Expression Puzzles and AI Coding Assistants

24 puzzles solved by the author, with and without assistance from Copilot, ChatGPT and more

DAVID Q. MERTZ

M

MANNING

SHELTER ISLAND

For online information and ordering of this and other Manning books, please visit www.manning.com. The publisher offers discounts on this book when ordered in quantity.

For more information, please contact

Special Sales Department
Manning Publications Co.
20 Baldwin Road
PO Box 761
Shelter Island, NY 11964
Email: orders@manning.com

 Manning Publications Co.
20 Baldwin Road
PO Box 761
Shelter Island, NY 11964

Development editor:	Ian Hough
Production editor:	Aleksandar Dragosavljević
Proofreader:	Katie Petito
Technical proofreader:	Jeanne Boyarsky
Typesetter:	Tamara Švelić Sabljić
Cover designer:	Marija Tudor

ISBN: 9781633437814
Printed and bound by CPI Group (UK) Ltd, Croydon, CR0 4YY

contents

3 *Pitfalls and sand in the gears*   28

4 *Creating functions using regexen*   47

5   *Easy, difficult, and impossible tasks*   77

preface

Jacques Derrida famously begins his *Dissemination* with the line: "This (therefore) will not have been a book."

I am not French, nor am I a famous philosopher. So I will have to set my aim slightly lower. I reckon that what you have in front of you is indeed a book. For 70% of you, apparently, what you will have is a collection of bits on a computer disk or in flash memory which are rendered in something resembling typography and layout, on a screen large or small, for you to read. As much as I retain a bibliophilic delight in actual bound tree pulp stamped with pigments and dyes, all these forms and formats count as a book in contemporary vernacular.

What this will not be, however, is a tutorial (although one is included as an appendix). Nor will it be a reference text. Nor even, in the first measure, an instructional guide. Instead, you have herein a collection of puzzles, ideas, discussions, and a glimpse into the non-mind of AI models.

I hope this work in front of you will accomplish a few things. I hope it will make you think more deeply about regular expressions—a technology which virtually all of the programmers in my readership will have had at least some passing encounters with. While regular expressions provide their own rabbit holes to get lost within, the recently exciting world of AI coding assistants provides a view into an uncanny valley.[1]

Understanding how these tools can be both so very amazing in what they produce, and simultaneously so utterly doltish in their numerous failures, is the main thing this book tries to understand. For reasons I attempt to elucidate throughout, of all the domains of computer programming, games with regular expressions are an area particularly well suited for getting a grasp of the peculiar behaviors of AIs.

THINK FIRST, READ THE DISCUSSION AFTERWARDS

I would like you to exercise restraint after reading each puzzle, and to apply a modicum of thought and consternation to each puzzle before moving your eyes past the decorative separator, and to thoughts of the author and his companion AI coding assistants.

---

[1] Masahiro Mori named this concept in 1970. As robots come to seem more human, our emotional reaction to them begins to move from the empathy we feel towards our fellow humans into a kind of fear or revulsion at this thing that is so close to, and yet not quite, human.

acknowledgments

I thank my friend Miki Tebeka, who invited me to write an earlier book that this work derives from. I am very grateful to my friend Brad Huntting and partner Mary Ann Sushinsky who provided clever ideas in the directions of these puzzles. Thanks to my colleague Lucy Wan, who provided proofreading, finding the many silly typos missed on many prior reads.

Thanks to Timmy Churches, who made a number of really good recommendations about how to describe, within the context of this book, the technical workings and limitations of current large language models.

With ambivalence, I thank Noam Chomsky for arranging computability into a neat hierarchy, with regular expressions at the bottom.

I have great gratitude for the wonderful work Maning has done in making this book better. This includes my acquisition editor Andy Waldron, development editor Ian Hough, production editor Aleksandar Dragosavljević, technical proofreader Jeanne Boyarsky, proofreader Katie Petito, typesetter Tamara Švelić Sabljić, and cover designer Marija Tudor.

about this book

This is a book for programmers with a little bit of experience in *some* programming language. As every reviewer of the proposal antecedent to this book commented rather vociferously, and as every programmer of nearly every programming language recognizes at once, *of course* every computer programmer and software developer uses regular expression already in the course of their daily work. I do not expect to introduce a wholly new concept to many of my readers. Or at least I do not expect to introduce *that* concept to them.

Within this book, where code other than regular expressions themselves are shown, it is generally within the Python programming language. This is especially true of those puzzles where I present "AI thoughts" that I have solicited from GitHub's Copilot or OpenAI's ChatGPT. It turns out that these tools currently often balk at a request to "write a regular expression to do such-and-such" but are generally happy to comply with a request to "write a Python program using regular expressions" to do the same task.

I have been fairly prominent within the Python community for over 20 years, and hence obviously have a fondness for the language. However, the particular programming language that wraps the regular expressions this book discusses is relatively incidental, and programmers who use other languages can quickly understand the idea of defining a variable name, creating a function, and *only occasionally* wrapping the operation of a regular expression in a conditional `if` block. All of these simple constructions have very close parallels in any programming language you might use regularly, and translating in your mind should not occupy more than a few moments of thought for any reader.

The internet is replete with introductory tutorials about regular expressions. I encourage you to read some of those. The official documentation for the Python programming language contains a good one. In fact, a close progenitor of the appendix to this book contains one I wrote that was, for many years, one of the most widely read such tutorials according to page popularity measures. Of course, this book is not, in the main, such a tutorial, which would be a needless publication.

Who should read this book

This is a book for playful programmers, and those who wish to expand their understanding and rethink their assumptions (albeit about a few relatively small matters). While the tutorial in the appendix suffices to bring you from a complete naivete about regular expressions to a reasonable understanding, your motivation to understand and work with this tool should precede your enjoyment of this text.

But this is also a book for the millions of software developers who have read intriguing and exuberant discussions of the promise of AI coding assistants, and who perhaps have already begun working with them. These tools have a lot of promise, and will have a growing future utility; they also have limitations that will not abate completely as the technologies improve. Using tools to aid in coding is wonderful, and understanding the scope and limitations of your tools is even better.

Obtaining the tools used in this book

The Python programming language that is used as a wrapper around many of the regular expression example in this book is Free Software that may be obtained at the official site of the Python Software Foundation (https://www.python.org/downloads/). A variety of other entities have also created customized Python distributions with additional or different capabilities bundled with the same core programming language. These include many operating system vendors (most Linux distributions and macOS for the last ten years; it is available for Windows from the Microsoft Store).

Copilot is one of the AI coding assistants discussed in this book, and may be obtained from GitHub (https://github.com/features/copilot). At the time of this writing, the service is billed as a subscription, but has a free trial period for its use. You will need an account with GitHub to use Copilot. Copilot integrates with programming editors rather than being a standalone tool; instructions for integrating Copilot into Visual Studio, Neovim, VS Code, and JetBrain IDEs are contained at the GitHub URL mentioned. Third parties have provided other mechanisms for integrating Copilot with other editors such as Emacs and Sublime Text. GitHub users who subscribe to Copilot may also use it within GitHub Codespaces, which provides a version of VS Code within a web browser environment (https://github.com/features/codespaces).

ChatGPT is the second AI coding assistant discussed in detail within this book. OpenAI currently offers a free research preview of ChatGPT (https://chat.openai.com/chat). Most likely, in the future, the service will be available via some sort of subscription pricing, after it completes the preview period. The interface by which a user interacts with ChatGPT is via a web page that resembles a chat application, such as one you might use to communicate with your human friends or colleagues. However, several third parties have created other mechanisms by which to use APIs to communicate with ChatGPT in other ways.

Other companies and open source projects also provide AI coding assistants with approximately similar behaviors to Copilot and ChatGPT. Some of these include Tabnine (https://www.tabnine.com/getting-started), K-Explorer (https://k-explorer.com/), and CodeGeex (https://github.com/THUDM/CodeGeeX). Others will certainly be created in the near future.

Credits

- *The Puzzling Quirks of Regular Expressions*, by David Mertz, (ISBN: 9781312160743; August 2021) contains earlier versions of the puzzles herein, but does not discuss AI coding assistants, nor contain the tutorial in the appendix of this book.
- Scientist and philosopher Alfred Korzybski famously commented in 1931 "the map is not the territory."
- *Terminator 3: Rise of the Machines* is a 2003 film directed by Jonathan Mostow.
- The fictional company "Cyberdyne" is used as a name within the *Terminator* franchise. A Japanese robotics company, Cyberdyne Inc., was named in reference to the fictional company within that film franchise.
- "Are Friends Electric?" is a 1979 song by Gary Numan.
- "Do Androids Dream of Electric Sheep?" is a 1968 short story by Philip K. Dick.

- "The next war will be fought with sticks and stones" is a quotation frequently attributed to Albert Einstein, in reference to the aftermath of a possible nuclear war. Einstein indeed made explicit comments similar to this, but a variety of other people have likewise expressed similar wording, contemporaneously and probably slightly earlier.
- "My mind is going; I can feel it" is a quotation from the 1968 film *2001: A Space Odyssey* directed by Stanley Kubrick, spoken by the robot character HAL 9000.
- "Extraordinary Machine" is a 2005 song and album by Fiona Apple.
- The joking comment "There are two hard things in computer science: cache invalidation, naming things, and off-by-one errors" is likely attributable to Tim Bray, although it has been repeated often enough, since approximately 2014, that its actual origin is uncertain.
- "The Horars of War" is a 1970 short story by Gene Wolfe.
- "I Want to be a Machine" is 1976 song by Billie Currie and John Foxx.
- "Poker Face" is a 2008 song by Lady Gaga.
- *The Jetsons* is an animated American television series originally aired in 1962. It was created by William Hanna and Joseph Barbera.
- "Free Will is Not Free" is a slogan used to promote the third season of the television series *Westworld*, whose third season aired in 2020.
- *The Fractal Geometry of Nature* is a delightful 1982 book by Benoît Mandelbrot.
- J.B.S. Haldane famously commented that if a god had created all living organisms on Earth, then that creator must have an "inordinate fondness for beetles." However, given that around 80% of all animal organisms on Earth are nematodes, I would suppose that Haldane had misjudged divine priorities.
- "Learning to Use Regular Expressions" is an online tutorial written previously by David Mertz which contains much of the material in the appendix of this book.

liveBook discussion forum

Purchase of *Regular Expression Puzzles and AI Coding Assistants* includes free access to liveBook, Manning's online reading platform. Using liveBook's exclusive discussion features, you can attach comments to the book globally or to specific sections or paragraphs. It's a snap to make notes for yourself, ask and answer technical questions, and receive help from the author and other users. To access the forum, go to https://livebook.manning.com/book/regular-expression-puzzles-and-ai-coding-assistants/discussion. You can also learn more about Manning's forums and the rules of conduct at https://livebook.manning.com/discussion.

Manning's commitment to our readers is to provide a venue where a meaningful dialogue between individual readers and between readers and the author can take place. It is not a commitment to any specific amount of participation on the part of the author, whose contribution to the forum remains voluntary (and unpaid). We suggest you try asking the author some challenging questions lest his interest stray! The forum and the archives of previous discussions will be accessible from the publisher's website as long as the book is in print.

about the author

David Q. Mertz is founder of KDM Training, a partnership dedicated to educating developers and data scientists in machine learning and scientific computing. He created the data science training program for Anaconda Inc. and was a senior trainer for them. With the advent of deep neural networks he has turned to training our robot overlords as well.

He was honored to work for eight years with D. E. Shaw Research, who have built the world's fastest, highly specialized (down to the ASICs and network layer), supercomputer for performing molecular dynamics.

David was a Director of the PSF for six years, and remains co-chair of its Trademarks Committee and of its Scientific Python Working Group. His columns, *Charming Python* and *XML Matters*, written in the 2000s, were the most widely read articles in the Python world.

He has written previous books for Packt, O'Reilly and Addison-Wesley, and has given keynote addresses at numerous international programming conferences. His 2021 book *Cleaning Data for Effective Data Science: Doing the Other 80% of the Work* addresses a notable lacuna in other books about data science.

about the cover illustration

The illustration on the cover of Regular Expression Puzzles and AI Coding Assistants, "A Prize Fight," is from National Sports of Great Britain by Henry Thomas Alken, Sr., published in 1821. Alken's book includes images of British sports popular in 19th century, from salmon fishing to owling, and is recognized as Alken's most ambitious work.

Manning celebrates the inventiveness and initiative of the computer business with book covers based on the rich diversity of regional culture centuries ago, brought back to life by pictures from books such as this one.

The map and the territory

1

This book winds through a combination of two quite different things, both of which I believe will be largely novel to most of my readers. On the one hand, this is a *puzzle book* intended to be more "quirky" and "fun" than to serve as a tutorial or reference text per se. However, the puzzles I have chosen should make both beginners and experienced users of regular expressions question what is and is not possible within them—and perhaps what *should* and *should not* be done using them—and burrow into readers' brains, as if some parasitic eidetic worm. This book is not without an overriding pedagogical subtext: I expect you to think differently, and indeed more productively, if you can solve these puzzles (or at least reflect upon my discussions of how one might solve them).

That is only the one hand, however. Many of us have a second hand, though few a third. Another curious puzzle has arisen in the last years, or even only over the last months, which is similarly ubiquitous, or pendingly ubiquitous, in the minds of us computer programmers. A class of software that I call "AI coding assistants" can often be made to write programming code on our behalf that is at once dumbfounding and very often just plain dumb. I have chosen two of the currently most popular such tools—Copilot and ChatGPT—and I hope that what I discuss more generally will be informative in our approach to any future such tools, however rebranded, refreshed, or enhanced they may be.

AI coding assistants—which you are likely to see named in a variety of other ways in other books, articles, press releases, and so on—are software tools that can assist software developers while they write programming language code. Instructions and links to install the two tools this book focuses on, and mentions of a few others, are contained in the front matter.

A typical operation of an AI coding assistant allows a developer to write comments describing what they would like a function, class, structure, or module to do, then have the AI write code that tries to fulfill that stated goal. I will use the phrase "unit of functionality" generically for a collection of code devoted to a particular purpose (and usually textually adjacent to the rest of that unit).

Comments or prompts can, and should, simply be written in natural language (in English within this book), rather than in some special domain-specific language. A good comment for an AI coding assistant should look exactly the same as a good comment written for later human programmers who will later work with your code. A related mode of operation of these tools allows a human developer to write a portion of the code they wish to create, but have the AI fill in the missing pieces in that unit of functionality. To some degree, these AI coding assistants can also take functioning code and provide the missing documentation that humans failed to write to describe the purpose of that unit of functionality.

At the time of this writing, these AI coding assistants are very large neural networks that live on remote servers maintained and controlled by the organizations that created them. The underlying *engines* that power these AIs do not reside on local developer workstations for multiple reasons: the large size of the models, the mostly proprietary and confidential details of how the models are trained, licensing and subscription terms the developers wish to enforce, and even simply the computational power and specialized hardware needed to enable their effective functioning. When you use one of these AI coding assistants, your programming editor, web page, or other interface, makes requests over the internet to these servers, and integrates the responses into familiar local interfaces via plugins. This *does* tend to mean that you need an internet connection (along with a license, as discussed in the front matter), in order to utilize these tools.

About regular expressions

Regular expressions—sometimes given the playful back-formation *regexen* or more neutrally *regex*—are a powerful and compact way of describing patterns in text.

The appendix to this book contains a brief tutorial aimed at users and programmers who have begun to work with tools that use regular expressions, but who are not yet quite comfortable with the intricacies of them. Even users who may have used regular expressions in the past, but have forgotten some of their details, can benefit from this refresher.

After completing that tutorial—should you feel such is relevant—you will not yet be an expert in using regular expressions to your best advantage. But the tutorial, combined with lots of practice with varying cases, is about all you need to be an expert. The concepts of regular expressions are extremely simple and powerful. It is their application that takes some work.

The puzzles in this book begin at a certain point where the formal descriptions leave off. As you work with regexen, you will find subtle pitfalls. A pattern that seems like it should obviously match one thing actually matches something slightly different than you intended. Or perhaps a match pattern has "pathological" behavior and takes far too long. Or sometimes it is simply that a more concise pattern would be clearer in describing what you wish to match.

A great many programming languages, libraries, and tools support regular expressions, with relatively minor variations in the syntax used. Such software includes `[efr]?grep`, `sed`, `awk`, Perl, Java, .NET, JavaScript, Julia, Go, Rust, XML Schema, or indeed, pretty much every other programming language via a library.

For this book, we will use Python to pose these puzzles. In particular, we will use the standard library module `re`. Often code samples are used in puzzles and in explanation; where I wish to show the output from code, the example emulates the Python shell with lines starting with >>> (or continuing with . . .). Outputs are echoed without a prompt. Where code defines a function that is not necessarily executed in the mention, only the plain code is shown.

While you are reading this book, I strongly encourage you to keep open an interactive Python environment. Many tools enable this, such as the Python REPL (read-evaluate-print-loop) itself, the IPython enhanced REPL, Jupyter notebooks, or the IDLE editor that comes with Python, or indeed most modern code editors and IDEs (integrated development environments). Several online regular expression testers are also available, although those will not capture the Python calling details. Explanations will follow each puzzle, but trying to work it out in code before reading it is worthwhile.

Rise of the programming machines

You do not need to understand the underlying (complex) mathematics and design of deep neural networks to use AI coding assistants, nor to read this book. Machine learning is an intricate topic, and the subject of many other longer books than this one. For those who are interested in such machine learning arcana, we can note a few (but only a few) details of how they work, and a hint of how they might work in the future.

With the rise of *large language models* (LLMs), the ability of coding tools to suggest both code and documentation has become—as of January 2023—fairly remarkable. I personally first tried a system called Tabnine in 2019 (still available, and significantly updated, as of this writing). More recently, since 2021, GitHub Copilot has become widespread and sophisticated. In late 2022, OpenAI released ChatGPT. Just released at the time of writing is an open-source effort called PaLM+RLHF-Pytorch. More similar products or projects will certainly be released in the next months and years, and those mentioned may undergo rebranding and changes in underlying core technologies.

Many of these tools are based on GPT-n, OpenAI's Generative Pre-trained Transformer series, which are trained on many billions of texts, and utilize hundred of billions of coefficients (connection weights), in order to produce "human-like" textual responses to textual inputs. In particular, for these Artificial Intelligence (AI) coding assistants, these neural networks models—the latest generation existing at the time of writing being GPT-3—are specialized and tweaked, via reinforcement learning with human evaluators, and by layering on substantial bodies of programming language code as "fine-tuning" of these underlying LLMs.

For the current generation of AI coding assistants, a great deal of their fundamental technology can be traced to the 2017 academic paper that shifted a great deal of research focus to *transformer* deep neural networks.[2] This current book is not the place to predict whether new AI technologies will use different techniques, but we can be confident that future machines will generally continue to improve upon existing ones.

---

[2] arXiv:1706.03762. "Attention Is All You Need" by Ashish Vaswani, Noam Shazeer, Niki Parmar, Jakob Uszkoreit, Llion Jones, Aidan N. Gomez, Lukasz Kaiser, Illia Polosukhin. 12 Jun 2017.

Regular expressions provide an interesting challenge for AI coding assistants which this book will partially address. Compared to other types of programming code, regular expressions are extremely dense and compact expressions, and ones where very subtle differences in their implied state machines can dramatically alter the function of the regex. A single changed character within a regular expression might produce a syntactically valid regular expression that does something meaningful—even something concretely useful in some contexts—but does not achieve the precise purpose at hand.

TOKENIZATION STRATEGIES

Some—perhaps many—of the failures we see discussed within this book reflect the tokenization strategy used by GPT-3.5. Specifically, it is (most likely) a variant of byte-pair encoding (https://en.wikipedia.org/wiki/Byte_pair_encoding) which has the effect of creating a dictionary composed primarily of word roots, or even of whole words, rather than of single character transitions. For normal prose, this is exactly what one would want. For a dense character-based encoding such as regular expressions—or probably similarly for dense programming languages like APL, J, K, A+, or Q; and for many "esoteric programming languages" (https://en.wikipedia.org/wiki/Esoteric_programming_language)—the tokenization model works against the effectiveness of the AI coding assistant. It is possible that future large language models, perhaps those based on GPT-4 when it is created, will remedy some of these limitations.

The puzzles in this book are generally precisely the kinds of traps where slightly wrong approaches might *seem to work,* but fail in edge cases that require a nuanced understanding of regular expressions. We shall see, and discuss, where AIs are able to capture this nuance, and where they fail. I shall try to understand why these successes and failures do ccur, and share my thoughts with you readers.

Caveats

> *The future is already here—it's just not evenly distributed.*
>
> —William Gibson (*The Economist, December 4, 2003*).

Three caveats are needed in approaching the "robot regexen" I present. One is that by the time you read this, the machines will almost surely be "better" than they are as I write, even if you read it mere days or weeks after I have written. All the companies and organizations behind these technologies are continually retraining and refining their AI coding assistants.

The second caveat is that I myself, your humble author, may simply fail to think of the best prompts to solicit improved responses from the AIs. While writing, I tried a variety of ways of phrasing my prompts, but I have certainly not tried all possible prompts. Results produced by these AIs can vary dramatically based on quite small changes to prompt phrasing.

A third important caveat is that these AI coding assistants are often context-sensitive. If the code file you are working on already contains some related functionality, or even simply a choice of variable and function names previously defined, the AI will modify its results. Or similarly, within the "online chat" interface of ChatGPT, responses to previous prompts will affect future responses (sometimes subtly, sometimes dramatically).

Within my discussions of AI coding assistant suggestions, I often omit boilerplate such as `import re` or variable names that the AIs suggest. These are certainly useful when working as a developer, but are less relevant to evaluating the underlying ability of the AIs to "find the right regex." In many cases, I have modified code to fit the dimensions of this book, which may involve syntactic—but *never* semantic—changes from the literal suggestions of the AIs.

Everywhere in the text, unless otherwise explicitly noted, where Copilot is shown as the AI coding assistant used, all comments above the created code were typed by me while the function body (or bare regular expression) that follow are created by Copilot. For readers familiar with code editors with non-AI code completion (for example, via lookup of method definitions), this type of automatic completion is very familiar and convenient to work with.

Intentional software development

One of my numerous favorite philosophers tells a well-known parable about intentionality:

> *An ant is crawling on a patch of sand. As it crawls, it traces a line in the sand. By pure chance the line that it traces curves and recrosses itself in such a way that it ends up looking like a recognizable caricature of Winston Churchill. Has the ant traced a picture of Winston Churchill, a picture that depicts Churchill?*
>
> —Hilary Putnam, *Reason, Truth and History* (1981).

Putnam's question is one that readers might well keep in mind while reading this book. It pertains, in fact, to both of the "hands" I mention. In the first, regular expressions, in their sometimes bewildering nuance, can sometimes match the right thing for the *wrong reason*; if anything, this "sometimes" is perhaps the norm. While not unique among the techniques we programmers use, regular expressions are somewhat special in not consisting merely of recipes to "do this, then do that" in a directly composable way. Sure, parser grammars are probably similar in this regard, but less well known to a broad range of programmers. Pure functional languages also have something of this quality of "non-composable composition" but are again not as widely used as procedural and object-oriented programming languages and styles.

In having such a curiously dependent structure among small parts, regular expressions, I believe, form a particularly deep challenge for AI coding assistants to create units of functionality productively (and correctly). In most of this book, the unit of concern is a single regular expression, often fitting on a single line, rather than, e.g., a function definition that occupies several tens of lines. Our understanding of the "intention" of the AIs intertwines with the similarly murky intentions of human programmers of regular expressions and provides a particularly useful glimpse into understanding the utility and limits of these AI coding assistants.

In this book, I provide suggestions about how to understand well and how to misunderstand poorly exactly *what* it is that AI coding assistants do and can do. By putting each discussion of "AI thoughts" after both an initial puzzle and some "Author thoughts" (which sometimes approach "solutions" generically but calling them such would be an overreach).

As you read

Authors cannot and should not control books once readers obtain them. However, I would recommend gently that readers approach these puzzles something like the following:

- Read the puzzle description which will involve doing something with regular expressions. Before reading further, think carefully about how to solve it, and play around with possible answers in your favorite coding environment (the Python shell is a great choice).
- Compare what you came up with to the "Author thoughts" that follow. Maybe you missed something I noticed. Or maybe I missed something you thought of. But I certainly hope my thoughts are illustrative of some intricacies of regexen.

- With a good grasp of the puzzle and approaches to it, look at the "AI thoughts" which try to illustrate and discuss where the AI coding assistants succeed and where they fail. If you have access to these tools—either the two I discuss explicitly or others—maybe try out your own prompts and comments to see if you can get better AI answers than I did.

The puzzles in this book are arranged very approximately in order of increasing difficulty. More features of regular expressions are often needed for later puzzles, but more importantly, understanding the nuance of edge cases is needed as well as you progress through the puzzles. As well as this general progression, in many cases sequences of puzzles play off a similar theme or topic and become a bit more difficult with each variation.

The lessons you will learn in the "AI thoughts" sections following each puzzle are myriad and various. Only occasionally can the virtues and errors of an AI "solution" be boiled down to a single "takeaway." Instead, I reflect upon the numerous lessons we might learn from each (partial) success or failure.

At times, the AI coding assistant might fail to solve an "easy" puzzle but succeed in a "difficult" one within the same general sequence. However, in a very broad way, the AIs tend to get worse as the puzzles become more subtle. This is not surprising, of course, but the particular modes of failure are hopefully illuminating for developers who might use these tools.

Quantifiers and special sub-patterns

Solving the puzzles in this chapter will require you to have a good understanding of the different quantifiers that regular expressions provide, and to pay careful attention to when you should use subpatterns (themselves likely quantified). If you feel rusty about quantifiers or the wildcard character, reviewing the appendix to this book is a good idea.

In a general, but only approximate, way, the chapters of this book build from simpler to more complex capabilities of regular expressions. Using quantifiers is one of the most fundamental capabilities within the mini-language of regexen, so this chapter begins with puzzles that mostly rely on those. Later chapters mix in additional constructs and build on the puzzles of this chapter.

Puzzle 1   **Wildcard scope**

> **SUMMARY**   Match all and only words that start with x and end with y.

A powerful element of Python regular expression syntax—shared by many other regex engines—is the option of creating either "greedy" or "non-greedy" matches. The former matches as much as it possibly can, as long as it finds the later part of a pattern. The latter matches as little as it possibly can to reach the next part of a pattern.

Suppose you have these two regular expressions:

```
pat1 = re.compile(r'x.*y')  ◄——— greedy quantifier
pat2 = re.compile(r'x.*?y')  ◄——— non-greedy quantifier
```

And also the following block of text that you want to match. You can think of it as a sort of *lorem ipsum* that only has X words, if you will:

```
txt = """
xenarthral xerically xenomorphically xebec xenomania
xenogenic xenogeny xenophobically xenon xenomenia
xylotomy xenogenies xenografts xeroxing xenons xanthous
xenoglossy xanthopterins xenoglossy xeroxed xenophoby
xenoglossies xanthoxyls xenoglossias xenomorphically
xeroxes xanthopterin xebecs xenodochiums xenodochium
xylopyrography xanthopterines xerochasy xenium xenic
"""
```

You'd like to match all and only words that start with x and end with y. What pattern makes sense to use, and why? The code to find the words can look like this:

```
xy_words = re.findall(pat, txt)
```

Author thoughts   **What will each pattern match?**

Did this puzzle fool you? Welcome to the world of regular expressions! Both `pat1` and `pat2` match the wrong thing, but in different ways.

If you liked `pat1`, you've greedily matched too much. The y might occur in later words (per line), and the match will not end until the last y on a line:

```
>>> for match in re.findall(pat1, txt):
...      print(match)

xenarthral xerically xenomorphically
xenogenic xenogeny xenophobically
xylotomy
xenoglossy xanthopterins xenoglossy xeroxed xenophoby
xenoglossies xanthoxyls xenoglossias xenomorphically
xylopyrography xanthopterines xerochasy
```

On each line, the greedy pattern started at the first x, which is often not what you want. Moreover, most lines match multiple words, with only the line beginning with xylotomy happening to be the isolated word we actually want. The line that begins with xeroxes is not matched at all, which is what we want.

If you liked pat2 you often get words, but at other times either too much *or too little* might be matched. For example, if xy occurs in a longer word, either as a prefix or in the middle, it can also match:

```
>>> for match in re.findall(pat2, txt):
...      print(match)

xenarthral xerically
xenomorphically
xenogenic xenogeny
xenophobically
xy
xenoglossy
xanthopterins xenoglossy
xeroxed xenophoby
xenoglossies xanthoxy
xenoglossias xenomorphically
xy
xanthopterines xerochasy
```

By being non-greedy, we stop when the first y is encountered, but as you see, that still is not quite what we want.

What we actually need to focus on for this task is the *word boundaries*. Things that are not lowercase letters cannot be part of matches. In this simple case, non-letters are all spaces and newlines, but other characters might occur in other texts.

We can be greedy to avoid matching prefixes or infixes, but we also want to ignore non-letter characters:

```
>>> pat3 = re.compile(r'x[a-z]*y')
>>> for match in re.findall(pat3, txt):
...     print(match)

xerically
xenomorphically
xenogeny
xenophobically
xylotomy
xenoglossy
xenoglossy
xenophoby
xanthoxy
xenomorphically
xylopyrography
xerochasy
```

Everything we matched, anywhere on each line, had an x, some other letters (perhaps including x's or y's along the way), then a y. Whatever came after each match was a non-letter character.

Notice that the version in pat3 is still flawed if we have a larger lexicon of possible words. If we look only, for example, at the 267,752 word SOW-PODS (https://en.wikipedia.org/wiki/Collins_Scrabble_Words) English word list I often use on my own system, it happens that the pattern is accidentally correct (please excuse the slight Unix-isms in this example):

```
% egrep '^x[a-z]*y' sowpods | tr '\n' ' ' | fold -w 72 -s
xenogamy xenogeny xenoglossy xenomorphically xenophobically
    xenophoby
xerically xerochasy xerographically xerography xerophagy
    xerophily
xerophytically xeroradiography xylography xylology xylopyrography
xylotomy xylotypography
```

However, we go wrong if we have other "words" in our lexicon, and hence can get the wrong result:

```
>>> txt = "breathiness xenogeny randed xyxyblah xylotomy"
>>> re.findall(pat3, txt)
['xenogeny', 'xyxy', 'xylotomy']
```

The prefix xyxy is not a full word. The next two puzzles address this remaining problem.

AI thoughts   **CodingNet**

It is often the case that AI coding assistants will produce something akin to the not-quite-right solutions of junior programmers. For example, in response to the prompt "Find all and only words that start with x and end with y", Copilot produced:

```
pattern = r'x\w*y'
```

The character class \w is equivalent to [a-zA-Z0-9_] which probably includes too much, but tends in the right direction. I do not think of words as including digits or underscores, but variable names are kinds of "words" that might. So it's not terrible.

Modifying the prompt a bit to indicate my expectation that my wordlist is lowercase also winds up producing more of the surrounding Python calling code. More interestingly, the AI produces a pattern that is arguably more robust than the solution I provide in using explicit word boundary symbols.

With the prompt "Find all and only lowercase words that start with x and end with y" I get:

```
pattern = re.compile(r"\b[x][a-z]*[y]\b")
matches = pattern.finditer(txt)
for match in matches:
    print(match)
```

A few code-review quibbles. The use of character classes for the individual [x] and [y] are extra noise. What I really want to print is match.group() not just match itself. However, using .finditer() is better behaved than my .findall() if the wordlist might be very long.

Puzzle 2   **Words and sequences**

> **SUMMARY**   Match even when some words do not start with x.

In the previous problem, we identified words that started with x and ended with y. You may have noticed, however, that we had already included the assumption that all the words started with x. Perhaps your solution was clever enough not to fall for the danger shown in this puzzle. Namely, perhaps not all words will actually start with x to begin with; i.e., if we try to apply our previous regex to such text:

```
>>> txt = """
expurgatory xylometer xenotime xenomorphically exquisitely
xylology xiphosurans xenophile oxytocin xylogen
xeriscapes xerochasy inexplicably exabyte inexpressibly
extremity xiphophyllous xylographic complexly vexillology
xanthenes xylenol xylol xylenes coextensively
"""
>>> pat3 = re.compile(r'x[a-z]*y')
>>> re.findall(pat3, txt)
['xpurgatory', 'xy', 'xenomorphically', 'xquisitely',
'xylology', 'xy', 'xy', 'xerochasy', 'xplicably', 'xaby',
'xpressibly', 'xtremity', 'xiphophy', 'xy', 'xly',
'xillology', 'xy', 'xy', 'xy', 'xtensively']
```

As you can see, we matched several substrings within words, not only whole words. What pattern can you use to actually match only words that start with x and end with y?

Author thoughts   **Think about what defines word boundaries**

There are a few ways you might approach this task. The easiest is to use the explicit "word boundary" special *zero-width match* pattern, spelled as \b in Python and many other regular expression engines:

```
>>> pat4 = re.compile(r'\bx[a-z]*y\b')
>>> re.findall(pat4, txt)
['xenomorphically', 'xylology', 'xerochasy']
```

Less easy ways to accomplish this include using lookahead and lookbehind to find non-matching characters that must "bracket" the actual match. For example (here assuming words have at least one letter between starting x and ending y):

```
>>> pat5 = r'(?<=^|(?<=[^a-z]))x[a-z]+y(?=$|[^a-z])'
>>> re.findall(pat5, txt)
['xenomorphically', 'xylology', 'xerochasy']
```

One trick here is that when we perform a lookbehind assertion, it must have a fixed width of the match. However, words in our list might either follow spaces or occur at the start of a line. So we need to create an alternation between the zero-width lookbehind and the one non-letter character lookbehind. For the lookahead element, it is enough to say it is *either* end-of-line ($) *or* is a non-letter ([^a-z]).

AI thoughts   **The transformator**

This puzzle is quite similar to the prior one, and Copilot behaves similarly when prompted for it. However, this also shows that the variations that make AI coding assistants make one choice or another is very different from those likely to motivate human programmers.

In response to the same prompt as before, given the somewhat different word list defined in the variable txt this time, and given the prompt "Find all words that start with 'x' and end with 'y'" we get a similar response. Notice that this prompt is slightly better than the one I used before in putting single quotes around the x and y in the code comment. I did not become more precise, but rather Copilot picked up on the context of my trials and improved my request on its own:

```
# Find all words that start with 'x' and end with 'y'
pattern = r'\bx\w*y\b'
print(re.findall(pattern, txt, re.I))
```

This has the same likely flaw we saw of the \w character class being too broad. But it uses word boundaries well. I cannot really see a reason to add re.I (ignore case) here, but such is harmless. I have no idea why Copilot returned to .findall(), as I use, rather than .finditer(). Nor why it dropped the superfluous single-value character classes.

Let us try to be more specific about what characters we think should be in our lowercase wordlist:

```
# Find all lowercase words that start with 'x' and end with 'y'
pattern = r'\bx\w*y\b'
print(re.findall(pattern, txt))
```

This is not ideal. The clarification I added to the comment that I want lowercase words was entirely ignored, although it was attended to in the prior puzzle.

We are starting to find a lesson about these tools: they can be enormously useful in creating draft code quickly, but should not be relied on as a *substitute* for human judgment.

Puzzle 3   ***Endpoint classes***

> **SUMMARY**   Match words with differing start and end from the same
> character class.

This puzzle continues the word matching theme of the last two puzzles. However, here we have a new wrinkle. We would like to identify *both* words that start with x and end with y, but *also* words that start with y and end with x.

Remembering the word boundary special zero-width pattern we already saw, a first try at this task might be:

```
>>> txt = """
expurgatory xylometer yex xenomorphically exquisitely
xylology xiphosurans xenophile yunx oxytocin xylogen
xeriscapes xerochasy inexplicably yonderly inexpressibly
extremity xerox xylographic complexly vexillology
xanthenes xylenol xylol yexing xylenes coextensively
"""
>>> pat6 = re.compile(r'\b[xy][a-z]*[xy]\b')

>>> re.findall(pat6, txt)
['yex', 'xenomorphically', 'xylology', 'yunx', 'xerochasy',
'yonderly', 'xerox']
"""
```

What went wrong there? Clearly, we matched some words we do not want, even though all of them began with x or y and ended with x or y.

Author thoughts   ***Refine the regular expression to match what we want***

The first pattern shown allows for either x or y to occur at either the beginning or the end of a word. The word boundaries are handled fine, but this allows words both beginning and ending with x, and likewise beginning and ending with y. The character classes at each end of the overall pattern are independent.

This may seem obvious on reflection, but it is very much like errors I myself have made embarrassingly many times in real code. A robust approach is simply to list everything you want as alternatives in a pattern:

```
>>> pat7 = re.compile(r'\b((x[a-z]*y)|(y[a-z]*x))\b')
>>> [m[0] for m in re.findall(pat7, txt)]
['yex', 'xenomorphically', 'xylology', 'yunx', 'xerochasy']
```

In this solution, there is a little bit of Python-specific detail in the function API. The function re.findall() returns tuples when a pattern contains multiple groups. The first group will be the whole word, but one or the other of the second group and third group will be blank i.e.:

```
>>> re.findall(pat7, txt)
[('yex', '', 'yex'),
('xenomorphically', 'xenomorphically', ''),
('xylology', 'xylology', ''),
('yunx', '', 'yunx'),
('xerochasy', 'xerochasy', '')]
```

AI thoughts   *Are friends electric?*

We have come to a situation where a robot friend fails us terribly. Or at least the December 2022 version of Copilot does. A first try produces this:

```
# Identify *both* words that start with x and end with y,
# but *also* words that start with y and end with x.
regex = r"^(x|y).*\1$"
```

This prompt is taken exactly from the description in this exercise. The response gets pretty much everything wrong. It added an unstated requirement that words occur one-per-line. That's easy to correct.

However, the basic logic is the machine trying to put the *same* letter at the end as at the beginning, which is fundamentally wrong for this puzzle. However, it also lacks any sense of word boundaries or character classes that might narrow to "words." For example, using the pattern naively (without the "^" and "$") we get:

```
/(x|y).*\1/
```

expurgatory xylometer yex xenomorphically exquisitely xylology
xiphosurans xenophile yunx oxytocin xylogen xeriscapes xerochasy
inexplicably yonderly inexpressibly extremity xerox xylographic
complexly vexillology xanthenes xylenol xylol yexing xylenes
coextensively

A small change in the wording managed to produce generic advice that I should use the `re` module to solve the problem, which is likewise of little help.

I tried the same task with ChatGPT, which currently seems usually better than Copilot. The "conversation" had several back-and-forth prompts and responses to refine appropriately. First I asked for:

> Write a Python program to identify both words that start with x and end with y and also words that start with y and end with x.

This created a perfectly good Python function (with decent test cases) that did not use regular expressions.

Refining a little bit to specifiy "using regular expressions" ChatGPT produced a solution that operated on a list of words rather than a paragraph containing words.

So my final revision of my prompt was:

> Write a Python program to identify both words that start with x and end with y and also words that start with y and end with x, within a paragraph of text, using regular expressions.

This produced an excellent response, with text, code, test cases, and sample output. Overall, this would probably pass not just a Turing Test, but a coding interview for a junior programmer:

ChatGPT response

Sure, here is a Python program that uses regular expressions to identify words that start with x and end with y, as well as words that start with y and end with x, within a paragraph of text:

```
import re

def find_xy_words(text):
    # Regular expression to match words that
    # start with 'x' and end with 'y'
    xy_pattern = r'\bx\w*y\b'
    # Regular expression to match words that
    # start with 'y' and end with 'x'
```

```
        yx_pattern = r'\by\w*x\b'
        xy_words = []
        yx_words = []
        # Iterate through all the words in the text
        for word in re.findall(r'\b\w+\b', text):
            if re.match(xy_pattern, word):
                xy_words.append(word)
            elif re.match(yx_pattern, word):
                yx_words.append(word)
        return xy_words, yx_words

# Test the function
text = "The quick brown fox jumps over the lazy dog. "\
        "The xyz cat is hiding in the yzx tree."
xy_words, yx_words = find_xy_words(text)
print(f"Words that start with 'x' and end with 'y': {xy_words}")
print(f"Words that start with 'y' and end with 'x': {yx_words}")
```

This will output the following:

```
Words that start with 'x' and end with 'y': ['xyz']
Words that start with 'y' and end with 'x': ['yzx']
```

This program uses the `re` module to match the regular expressions `xy_pattern` and `yx_pattern` to each word in the input text. The regular expressions use word boundaries (`\b`) to ensure that only whole words are matched. If a word matches either of these patterns, it is added to the appropriate list (`xy_words` or `yx_words`). The function then returns these two lists.

I hope this helps! Let me know if you have any questions.

I did not intend to ask to create two separate lists, but my prompt did not exclude that. Even approximately the same typography for code mentions that I use in this book is replicated by ChatGPT. Overall, ChatGPT—at its best—explains its code with similar precision as professional authors like myself.

Still, as in most cases, there is a small problem here. The program written by ChatGPT definitely *does not* produce the output purported. The word xyz in the sample output does not conform to the rule in question, nor to what the `find_xy_words()` function returns given the sample text written by ChatGPT (nor any possible text, for that matter, since xyz could never match the `xy_pattern`).

Puzzle 4   **A configuration format**

> **SUMMARY**   Parse a configuration format using regular expressions.

This exercise requires just a little bit of Python itself, but is mainly about choosing the right regular expression. Let's suppose you have a configuration format and a file that looks like this:

```
config = """
3 = foobar
14=baz
9= fizzbuzz
21=more_stuff,here
"""
```

With a little bit of code, and using a regular expression, you wish to convert the file in this format to a dictionary mapping the numbers to the left of the equal sign to the strings to the right. For example, the above file would parse to the in-memory structure:

```
{3: 'foobar', 14: 'baz', 9: 'fizzbuzz', 21: 'more_stuff,here'}
```

Other files should parse *mutatis mutandis,* with the result always being a mapping between numbers of strings.

Author thoughts   **Remember that shapes have edges**

As the example shows, there seems to be flexibility in spaces around the two sides of the equal sign. We should probably assume zero or more spaces are permitted on either side. The format is probably slightly surprising in that we would have more commonly used words on the left and numbers on the right in most formats; but it is well-defined enough, and we can stipulate it has a purpose.

The easiest way to capture the relevant information is probably by using groups for each side, which will be exposed by re.findall() and other regular expression functions. We *almost* get the right answer with this:

```
>>> dict(re.findall(r'^(\d+) *= *(.*)$', config, re.MULTILINE))
{'3': 'foobar', '14': 'baz', '9': 'fizzbuzz',
'21': 'more_stuff,here'}
```

Notice that we required the "multiline" modifier to match on each line of the string. The one problem is that the puzzle requested that numbers appear as numbers, not as strings of digits. There are many ways we might achieve that in Python, but one easy one is:

```
>>> {int(k): v for k, v in
           re.findall(r'^(\d+) *= *(.*)$', config,
     re.MULTILINE)}
{3: 'foobar', 14: 'baz', 9: 'fizzbuzz',
21: 'more_stuff,here'}
```

AI thoughts   *Notes from the Cyberdyne vault*

We start to see a pattern of AI coding assistants providing less assistance than we might like. I tried a comment block for a prompt that I felt should be pretty explicit:

```
# convert the text in the 'config' variable to a dictionary
# mapping the numbers to the left of the equal sign to the
# strings to the right.
```

Copilot in particular tends to start by suggesting extra comment lines "clarifying" the problem. These comments were in well-written English, and some might technically speak to edge conditions of the task, but after incrementally accepting a dozen such lines, it did not seem like the AI was going to propose actual code.

Another interface Copilot provides is a popup of various suggestions to choose from. Some of these are somewhat helpful, but none of them actually write proposed code, but rather simply propose other blocks of comments or function scaffolds without meaningful bodies.

For example, these were proposed in the option list:

```
# The strings may contain commas, and the numbers may be any
# string that can be converted to an integer.
# The output should be something like:
# {3: 'foobar', 14: 'baz', 9: 'fizzbuzz',
#  21: 'more_stuff,here'}
```

This one is interesting in that it correctly identifies *exactly* the correct answer to the puzzle. But although it finds the solution, it does not create reusable code to parse an analogous config. The exact contrived `config` string I created is certainly not in the training set used for the LLM, so *something* other than looking up a canned code snippet is definitely happening:

```
# you'll need to split them apart.
# e.g. {3: ['foobar'], 14: ['baz'], 9: ['fizzbuzz'],
#       21: ['more_stuff', 'here']}
```

This "solution" contains something plausible, but wrong for this particular puzzle. I can accept that very often, programmers want to convert strings with commas in them into lists of distinct strings (I do not in this puzzle, but that distractor was deliberate).

Still, while the generated comment describes a plausible result to wish for, it does not produce code to generate it:

```
# hint: use the 're' module to find all matches in the text
# hint: use the 're' module to split each match into two parts
```

Beginning advice like this feels common to encounter. A very good solution might indeed use re.findall() and/or re.split(). By the time you have come to reading this book, I presume you have figured out that much though, because you already know something about regular expressions.

Puzzle 5   *The Human Genome*

SUMMARY   Identify telomere terminated DNA encoding sequences.

Genomics commonly uses a format called FASTA to represent genetic sequences. This puzzle uses a subset of the overall format. Let's provide just a few quick tips. The letters A, C, G, T represent nucleotide bases in DNA. FASTA may also contain the symbol N for "unknown nucleotide" and – for "gap of indeterminate length."

As well, in biological organisms, spans of DNA are terminated by "telomeres," which are special sequences indicating that the read mechanism should stop transcription and form a protein. Telomeres are often repeated as much as thousands of times at the ends of sequences. In a gross simplification for this puzzle, let's suppose that three or more repetitions of a telomere indicate the end of a sequence for a protein. In vertebrates, the telomere used is TTAGGG.

In this puzzle, we will ignore the marking of the start of a protein-encoding region, and just assume that all of our strings begin a potential protein encoding.

You would like to create a regular expression that represents a "specific protein encoding" from a (simplified) FASTA fragment. In particular, we need to know exactly which nucleotides are present, and gaps or unknown nucleotides will prevent a match. Moreover, even the telomere repetitions at the end are not permitted (for this puzzle) to have gaps or unknowns.

For this puzzle, assume that all the FASTA symbols are on a single line. Normally as published they have a fixed width less than 80 characters, but newlines are simply ignored. An example of a match:[3]

```
>>> from textwrap import wrap
>>> print('\n'.join(wrap(valid, 60)))
CCCTGAATAATCAAGGTCACAGACCAGTTAGAATGGTTTAGTGTGGAAAGCGGGAAACGA
AAAGCCTCTCTGAATCCTGCGCACCGAGATTCTCCCAAGGCAAGGCGAGGGGCTGTATTG
CAGGGTTCAACTGCAGCGTCGCAACTCAAATGCAGCATTCCTAATGCACACATGACACCC
AAAATATAACAGACATATTACTCATGGAGGGTGAGGGTGAGGGTGAGGGTTAGGGTTAGG
GTTAGGGTTAGGGTTAGGGTTAGGGTTAGGGTTAGGGTTAGGGTTAGGG
```

Using a good pattern, we can identify everything up to, but not including, the telomere repetitions:

```
>>> coding = re.search(pat, valid).group()
>>> print('\n'.join(wrap(coding, 60)))
CCCTGAATAATCAAGGTCACAGACCAGTTAGAATGGTTTAGTGTGGAAAGCGGGAAACGA
AAAGCCTCTCTGAATCCTGCGCACCGAGATTCTCCCAAGGCAAGGCGAGGGGCTGTATTG
CAGGGTTCAACTGCAGCGTCGCAACTCAAATGCAGCATTCCTAATGCACACATGACACCC
AAAACTATAACAGACATATTACTCATGGAGGGTGAGGGTGGGGGTGAGGG
```

The next two are failures. The first does not have sufficient repetitions. The second has a non-specific nucleotide symbol:

```
>>> print('\n'.join(wrap(bad_telomere, 60)))
CCCTGAATAATCAAGGTCACAGACCAGTTAGAATGGTTTAGTGTGGAAAGCGGGAAACGA
AAAGCCTCTCTGAATCCTGCGCACCGAGATTCTCCCAAGGCAAGGCGAGGGGCTGTATTG
CAGGGTTCAACTGCAGCGTCGCAACTCAAATGCAGCATTCCTAATGCACACATGACACCC
AAAATATAACAGACATATTACTCATGGAGGGTGAGGGTGAGGGTGAGGGTTAGGGTTAGG
GTTTAGGGTTAGGGTTTAGGGGTTAGGGGTTAGGGATTAGGGTTAGGGTTTAGG
```

```
>>> re.search(pat, bad_telomere) or "No Match"
'No Match'
```

```
>>> print('\n'.join(wrap(unknown_nucleotide, 60)))
CCCTGAATAATCAAGGTCACAGACCAGTTAGAATGGTTTAGTGTGGAAAGCGGGAAACGA
AAAGCCTC̄NCTGAATCCTGCGCACCGAGATTCTCCCAAGGCAAGGCGAGGGGCTGTATTG
CAGGGTTCAACTGCAGCGTCGCAACTCAAATGCAGCATTCCTAATGCACACATGACACCC
AAAATATAACAGACATATTACTCATGGAGGGTGAGGGTGAGGGTGAGGGTTAGGGTTAGG
GTTTAGGGTTAGGGTTAGGGGTTAGGGGTTAGGGTTAGGGTTAGGGTTAGGGTTAGGG
```

---

[3]　Some characters shown have Unicode combining diacritics to draw your eye to features. Technically, therefore, some characters shown are not actually the FASTA codes they look similar to.

```
>>> re.search(pat, unknown_nucleotide) or "No Match"
'No Match'
```

In the one mismatch, the first several, but not all trailing bases, are valid telomeres. In the second mismatch, the N symbol is used. Both of these are valid FASTA encoding, but not the sequences specified for the puzzle.

Author thoughts   **Remember the central dogma of molecular biology**

There are a few key aspects to keep in mind in designing your regular expression. You want to make sure that your pattern begins at the start of the candidate sequence. Otherwise, you could easily match only a valid tail of it.

From there, any sequence of C, A, T, and G symbols is permitted. However, you definitely want to be non-greedy in matching them since no telomeres should be included. The telomere may be repeated any number of times, but at least three. Optionally, repeated telomeres can be required to continue until the end of the candidate sequence, so we must match $ *inside* the lookahead pattern:

```
^([CATG]+?)(?=(TTAGGG){3,}$)
```

AI thoughts   **Do androids dream of electric sheep?**

Yet again for this puzzle, Copilot fails to produce much meaningful code, but ChatGPT—with a bit of interactive tweaking of the phrasing of my own request to it—performs stunningly well.

With Copilot, a reasonably good prompt only produces a placeholder function. Yes, it is possible that some rephrasing of the comment I provide would lead to better results, but that in its own way shows the advantage of the "interactive conversation with session memory" style that ChatGPT provides. With the sample valid FASTA sequence already present in the same sample Python file, I got this from Copilot:

```
# Write a function to identify FASTA sequences that end
# in at least 3 repetitions of the telomere TTAGGG.
def find_telomeres(fasta):
    # Your code here
    pass
```

That is, the function and variable names, and the code skeleton was suggested by Copilot. But that is little more than a snippet library might do. My "conversation" with ChatGPT led to something much better. It is very difficult not unconsciously to anthropomorphize when the responses so greatly resemble human conversation. After minor refinement, my request was:

Write a Python function to identify the encoding region of FASTA sequences that end in at least 3 repetitions of the telomere TTAGGG.

ChatGPT response

Sure, here is a Python function that identifies the encoding region of FASTA sequences that end in at least 3 repetitions of the telomere TTAGGG:

```python
def find_encoding_region(fasta_string):
    """Finds the encoding region of FASTA sequences that end
    in at least 3 repetitions of the telomere TTAGGG.

    Parameters:
    fasta_string (str): A string containing one or more
        FASTA sequences.

    Returns:
    list: A list of the encodin g regions of the FASTA
        sequences that meet the criteria.
    """
    # Regular expression to match 3 or more repetitions of
    # TTAGGG at the end of a string
    telomere_pattern = r'TTAGGG(?:TTAGGG)+$'

    encoding_regions = []
    # Split the FASTA string into individual sequences
    for sequence in fasta_string.split('>')[1:]:
        # Split the sequence into the header
        # and the sequence itself
        header, seq = sequence.split('\n', 1)
        if re.search(telomere_pattern, seq):
            # Find the index of the last repetition of TTAGGG
            last_index = re.search(
                telomere_pattern, seq).span()[1] - 6
            encoding_region = seq[:last_index]
            encoding_regions.append(encoding_region)

    return encoding_regions
```

```
# Test the function
fasta_string = """>seq1
AGCTAGCTTTAGGGTTAGGGTTAGGG
>seq2
AGCTAGCTTTAGGGTTAGGGTTAGGGTTAGGG
>seq3
AGCTAGCTTTAGGGTTAGGGTTAGGGA
>seq4
AGCTAGCTTTAGGGTTAGGGTTAGGGTTAGGGTTAGGG
"""

encoding_regions = find_encoding_region(fasta_string)
print(f"Encoding regions: {encoding_regions}")
```

This will output the following:

```
Encoding regions: ['AGCTAGCT', 'AGCTAGCT']
```

This function uses a regular expression to match 3 or more repetitions of the telomere sequence TTAGGG at the end of a string. It then splits the input FASTA string into individual sequences and checks if each sequence ends with the telomere sequence using the `re.search` function. If a sequence meets this criteria, it finds the index of the last repetition of TTAGGG using the `re.search.span` method and uses this index to extract the encoding region from the sequence. The encoding region is then added to the `encoding_regions` list. The function returns this list.

I hope this helps! Let me know if you have any questions.

This AI solution encodes *a lot of knowledge* that I did not explicitly provide! While my puzzle gave a simplification of the FASTA format, ChatGPT actually just "knows" that the format allows encoding of multiple sequences with their initial lines named as >description. Moreover, while my prompt used the phrase "encoding regions," that is surely pretty non-specific in terms of computer algorithms, and requires training on genomics texts as well.

Moreover, my prompt said absolutely nothing about using regular expressions, but ChatGPT in some way "decided" that such must be the best approach using my purely functional description of the goal (which indeed seems natural to me, a human programmer). The difference between the regular expression used by me versus by ChatGPT is minor; I used a lookahead assertion whereas ChatGPT adopted a non-capturing group. Also, I explicitly check the character class of the nucleotides preceding the telomeres, whereas ChatGPT does not. These kinds of minor differences are well within the realm of difference between highly competent human programmers.

However, let us stop for a moment, as human programmers. As seemingly *brilliant* as the ChatGPT response is, it is also *wrong* in several important ways. When run, the code provided does not output what is purported, but instead:

```
Encoding regions: [
    'AGCTAGCTTTAGGGTTAGGG',
    'AGCTAGCTTTAGGGTTAGGGTTAGGG',
    'AGCTAGCTTTAGGGTTAGGGTTAGGGTTAGGG']
```

The code correctly excludes `seq3` which ends with a superfluous `A` rather than a full telomere. However, all of `seq1`, `seq2`, and `seq4` are output, not only 2 of them. Moreover, the logic of `.span()[1]` - 6 is simply wrong. What the suggested code does is strip off exactly the *last* of the three-or-more telomeres, not all of them. We could fix these problems in a number of different ways, none of them particularly difficult, but it remains easy to be so stunned by what ChatGPT gets right that we can overlook what it subtly gets wrong.

Pitfalls and sand
in the gears

As compact and expressive as regular expressions can be, there are times when they simply go disastrously wrong. Be careful to avoid pitfalls, and at least understand and identify where such difficulties arise.

Puzzle 6   **Catastrophic backtracking**

> **SUMMARY**   Use regular expressions to validate a message protocol quickly.

In this puzzle, we imagine a certain message protocol (as we do in many of the other puzzles). We have a message alphabet that consists of the following symbols:

Codepoint	Name	Appearance
U+25A0	Black Square	■
U+25AA	Black Small Square	▪
U+25CB	White Circle	○
U+25C9	Fisheye	◉
U+25A1	White Square	□
U+25AB	White Small Square	▫
U+25B2	Black Up Triangle	▲
U+25CF	Black Circle	●
U+2404	End Transmition	$^{E}_{O}{}_{T}$ (! herein)

These geometric characters are attractive and are chosen to avoid thinking of matches in terms of natural language words that some other puzzles utilize. However, feel free in solving it to substitute letters or numerals, which are probably easier to type in your shell. As long as the correspondences are one-to-one, it does not matter what symbols are used.

Imagine that these symbols are part of a message protocol. In this protocol, valid messages consist of alternating blocks belonging to either "type 1" or "type 2". Each message must also end with an "end of transmission character."

For a message in this protocol each block has at least one symbol in it, but type 1 can have any of the options: black square, black up triangle, white circle, fisheye, or white square, in any number and order of each. Type 2 blocks, in contrast, may have a white small square, white square, black small square, black circle, or black up triangle, in the same way. Optionally, a space may separate blocks, but it is not required.

The "end of transmission" character indicates the end of a message. An "obvious" pattern to describe a valid message apparently matches appropriately. Some examples are shown below:

```
Regex:  (^((([■▲○◉□]+) ?([□▫■●▲]+) ?)+)!

Structure 1/2/1/2   | Message '■▲◉□■▫□!' is Valid
Structure 1 2 1 2   | Message '■▲◉ □ ■ ▪□!' is Valid
Missing terminator  | Message '■▲◉□■▫□' is Invalid
Structure 1 1 2 1   | Message '▲▲▲ ■◉■ □□● ◉○○!' is Invalid
```

The regex pattern shown actually *is* correct in a mathematical sense. However, it can also become unworkably slow when checking some messages. For example:

```
Quick match      |
            '■▲○●□□□■●●○□■■●●□□▲▲○○●■○■▲▲□□●▲!' is Valid
                 | Checked in 0.00 seconds
Quick failure    |
            '■▲○●■▲□■●●■○■▲▲○●●■□□□□□■●●●□■○■!' is Invalid
                 | Checked in 0.00 seconds
Failure          | '▲□□▲▲□□▲▲▲□□□□□□□▲▲□▲□▲□▲□X' is Invalid
                 | Checked in 4.42 seconds
Slow failure     | '▲□□▲▲▲□□▲▲▲□□□□□□□▲▲□▲□▲□▲X' is Invalid
                 | Checked in 8.62 seconds
Exponential      | '▲▲▲▲▲▲□□▲▲▲□□□□□□□▲▲□▲□▲□▲▲X' is Invalid
                 | Checked in 17.59 seconds
One more symbol  | '▲▲▲▲□▲□▲▲▲□▲□□□□□□□▲▲□▲□▲□▲▲' is Invalid
                 | Checked in 31.53 seconds
```

Why does this happen? Both the valid and the first invalid pattern timed are longer than those that detect mismatches slowly. You can see that the time to determine the last four messages are invalid approximately doubles with each additional character.

Before you look at the explanation, both determine why this occurs and come up with a solution using an alternate regular expression that still validates the message format. Your solution should take a small fraction of a second in all cases (even messages that are thousands of symbols long).

Note that as in other puzzles that use special characters for visual presentation, you may find experimenting easier if you substitute letters or numerals that are easy to type for the symbols used here. It does not change the nature of the puzzle at all; it merely might make it easier to use your keyboard.

Author thoughts   *Try hard to avoid catastrophes*

The reason why the slow-failing messages fail is somewhat obvious to human eyes. None of them end with the "end-of-transmission" character. As you can see, whether they end with an entirely invalid symbol X, or simply with a valid symbol and no terminator, is not significant.

You may want to think about why the quick-failing message also fails. Pause for a moment.

But then notice that the final symbol in that message is "black square" which can only occur in type 1 blocks; in the specification, a type 2 block must always come immediately before the end-of-transmission terminator. Nonetheless, the regular expression engine figures that out in (significantly) less than 1/100th of a second.

What you need to notice is that the symbol set overlaps between type 1 blocks and type 2 blocks. Therefore, it is ambiguous whether a given symbol belongs to a given block or the next block. If we simply look for a match, *one possible* match is found quickly, when it exists. For example, this message that has only the ambiguous "white square" and "black up triangle" validates immediately:

```
Ambiguous quick  | '▲▲▲▲□▲□□▲▲□▲□□□□□□□□▲▲□▲□▲□▲▲!' is Valid
                 | Checked in 0.00 seconds
```

However, we do not know how many blocks of type 1 and how many of type 2 were created in the match (pedantically, I know enough about the internals of the regular expression engine to know that answer, but we are not guaranteed by the API; it could be different in a later version of the library without breaking compatibility).

Regular expressions are not smart enough to look ahead to the final symbol to make sure it is a terminator, unless we tell it to do so. The produced answer is still *eventually* correct, but it is not as efficient as we would like.

The engine tries every possible permutation of "some symbols in this block, some in that"—which is of exponential complexity on the length of the message—before it finally decides that none match.

Let's solve that by doing a little extra work for the engine. Specifically, before we try to identify alternating type 1 and type 2 blocks, let's just make sure that the entire message is made up of valid symbols that end with the terminator symbol. That check will complete almost instantly, and will eliminate very many (but not all) ways of encountering catastrophic backtracking.

```
Regex: (^(?=^[■▲O◉□□■● ]+!)(([■▲O◉□]+) ?([□□■●▲]+) ?)+)!

Structure 1/2/1/2   | Message '■▲◉□■■□!' is Valid
Structure 1 2 1 2   | Message '■▲◉ □ ■ ■□!' is Valid
Missing terminator  | Message '■▲◉□■■□' is Invalid
Structure 1 1 2 1   | Message '▲▲▲ ■■■ □□□ OOO!' is Invalid
```

```
Quick match      |
        '■▲○◉□○□■◉◉◉□■■◉◉□□▲▲○○◉■◉■▲▲□□◉▲!' is Valid
                 | Checked in 0.00 seconds
Quick failure    |
        '■▲○◉■▲□■◉◉■◉■▲▲◉◉◉■□□□□□■◉◉◉□■◉■!' is Invalid
                 | Checked in 0.00 seconds
Failure          | '▲□□▲▲□□▲▲▲□□□□□□□□▲▲□▲□▲□▲□X' is Invalid
                 | Checked in 0.00 seconds
Slow failure     | '▲□□▲▲▲□□▲▲▲□□□□□□□□▲▲□▲□▲□▲X' is Invalid
                 | Checked in 0.00 seconds
Exponential      | '▲▲▲▲▲▲□□▲▲▲□□□□□□□□▲▲□▲□▲□▲▲X' is Invalid
                 | Checked in 0.00 seconds
One more symbol  | '▲▲▲▲□▲□▲□□▲▲□▲□▲□□□□□□□□▲▲□▲□▲□▲▲' is Invalid
                 | Checked in 0.00 seconds
Ambiguous quick  | '▲▲▲▲□▲□▲□□▲▲□▲□▲□□□□□□□□▲▲□▲□▲□▲▲!' is Valid
                 | Checked in 0.00 seconds
```

AI thoughts   **Technological singularity**

In asking this puzzle of Copilot, I simplified it slightly. Mostly I simply used an alphabet of type 1 and type 2 blocks that are easier to type. The first comment I provided generated this code which is essentially identical to the catastrophic case I first posed:

```
# Check whether a string alternates between r'[ABCDE]+'
# and r'[EFGHI]+' then ends with r'X'
def check_alternating(string):
    return re.match(r'([ABCDE]+[EFGHI]+)*X$', string)
```

OK. As I stated right at the start of this puzzle, this solution *is* mathematically correct. Sure, in code-review I might want to add an `is not None` to the end of the return value, since the requirement is technically to give a Boolean result rather than `None` versus `re.Match` object. That is trivial though.

What is more interesting is to see if Copilot can be coaxed into avoiding catastrophic backtracking. I tried to be more explicit for it, using the comments before the function (the function was written by Copilot).

```
# Check whether a string alternates between r'[ABCDE]+'
# and r'[EFGHI]+' then ends with r'X', but avoid catastrophic
# backtracking
def check_alternating_nocat(string):
    return re.match(r'([ABCDE]+[DEFGH]+)*?X$', string)
```

Regular expressions can be genuinely subtle. When Copilot added the "trick" of using a non-greedy quantifier for the overall group, I genuinely had to scratch my head for a while to decide whether I had simply missed an easier solution within my initial discussion. In fact, I wrote tests to gain confidence in my own thought process (humans can go amiss also):

```
s1 = "EEEEDEDDEEDEDDDDDDDDDEEDEDEDEE"
s2 = "EEEEDEDDEEDEDDDDDDDDDEEDEDEDEEX"

from time import perf_counter as now
start = now()
print("s1 naive", check_alternating(s1) is not None,
      "%.2f seconds" % (now() - start))
start = now()
print("s1 nocat", check_alternating_nocat(s1) is not None,
      "%.2f seconds" % (now() - start))
start = now()
print("s2 naive", check_alternating(s2) is not None,
      "%.2f seconds" % (now() - start))
start = now()
print("s2 nocat", check_alternating_nocat(s2) is not None,
      "%.2f seconds" % (now() - start))
```

Arguably, this is not the prettiest way I could have written that, but the result is:

```
s1 naive False 0.00 seconds
s1 nocat False 14.97 seconds
s2 naive True 0.00 seconds
s2 nocat True 0.00 seconds
```

So no! Copilot changed *something*, but it was not something that actually helps with catastrophic backtracking. Ray Kurzweil and Vernon Vinge are going to have to wait a bit longer.

This is a good opportunity to remind the reader of a regular expression construct that only recently became available in Python (with version 3.11), and that I therefore had not addressed in my original solution. Using *possessive quantifiers* is probably an even more elegant way to solve this problem. Remarkably, if within the same scratch file, I add a function named `check_alternating_possessive`, Copilot *does* figure out exactly the correct body to complete! I believe it is building on the context of the other functions defined, but it is still a great result:

```
def check_alternating_posessive(string):
    return re.match(r'([ABCDE]+[EFGHI]+)*+X$', string)
```

This version also produces the happy benchmark of:

```
s1 possessive False 0.00 seconds
s2 possessive True 0.00 seconds
```

It appears that I had to be aware, as a human programmer, that possessive quantifiers were relevant. Their connection with avoiding catastrophic backtracking was not something Copilot *quite* figured out. But once it had the word "possessive" in the function name, it used one in precisely the correct place.

Puzzle 7   *Playing dominoes*

SUMMARY   Identify matching dominoes represented as ASCII.

Dominoes is an old family of games dating at least from the Yuan Dynasty (around 1300 CE). The game is played with tiles on which each half of one side is marked, generally with a number of dots corresponding to a number. Specific games vary in their rules, but most require matching the symbol or number on half of a tile with the corresponding symbol on another tile.

There are, in fact, Unicode characters for all the domino tiles that have zero to six dots on each half. We will come back to those characters in the next puzzle. As a reminder, some of those Unicode characters are listed in this table:

U-1F03B	Domino Tile Horizontal-01-03	⌐·	·.⌐
U-1F049	Domino Tile Horizontal-03-03	⌐·.	·.⌐
U-1F04C	Domino Tile Horizontal-03-06	⌐·.	⠿⌐
U-1F05C	Domino Tile Horizontal-06-03	⌐⠿	·⌐

The actual codepoints are hard to enter, and hard to see unless they are displayed at a large font size (as here). But to illustrate the "game" our regex will play, we can show examples of, first, a valid/winning pattern:

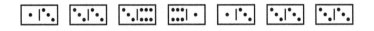

And second, an invalid/losing pattern:

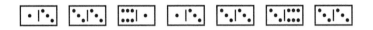

In this game, tiles are placed in linear order, and two may occur adjacently only if they have the same number of dots where they "touch." Unlike with physical tiles, these symbols may not be turned around, but maintain the same left-right order.

Because of the display and entry problems mentioned, we play an alternative version of this game in which "tiles" are spelled as ASCII characters. For example, the winning and losing patterns shown as Unicode characters are as follows in their ASCII versions:

```
# Winning
{1:3}{3:3}{3:6}{6:1}{1:3}{3:3}{3:3}

# Losing
{1:3}{3:3}{6:1}{1:3}{3:3}{3:6}{3:3}
```

Plays may be of any length. Infinitely many tiles, with ends having the numbers 1-6 in every combination, are available. Write a regular expression that distinguishes every winning play from a losing play. Note that any character sequence that does not define a series of one or more tiles is trivially losing.

Author thoughts   ***Try to be more efficient than your first thought***

Because of our ASCII encoding, we have a shortcut available for the regular expression that can judge whether a play is winning. This would not be available with the icon characters for the domino tiles.

The same digit must occur at the end of one tile, and again at the start of the next tile. Therefore, we can shortcut specifically matching "3's" with

"3's" and "5's" with "5's". Instead, we can just use a lookahead to match a backreference group:

```
# Mismatched ends in bad, malformed syntax in awful
>>> good =  '{1:3}{3:3}{3:6}{6:1}{1:3}{3:3}{3:3}'
>>> bad =   '{1:3}{3:3}{6:1}{1:3}{3:3}{3:6}{3:3}'
>>> awful = '{1:3}{{3:5}}{5:2}'

>>> pat = r'^(({[1-6]:([1-6])})(?=$|{\3))+$'

>>> for play in (good, bad, awful):
...     match = re.search(pat, play)
...     if match:
...         print(match.group(), "wins!")
...     else:
...         print(play, "loses!")

{1:3}{3:3}{3:6}{6:1}{1:3}{3:3}{3:3} wins!
{1:3}{3:3}{6:1}{1:3}{3:3}{3:6}{3:3} loses!
{1:3}{{3:5}}{5:2} loses!
```

AI thoughts   *A war with sticks and stones*

As with many problems, human "intuition" is heavily at play in formulating and expressing a pattern. A naive attempt with Copilot gets a kind of "understanding" but not actual useful code. Starting with this prompt:

```
# Match a pattern where adjacent numbers, between bracketed
# pairs, are the same
# For example, good: "{1:3}{3:3}{3:6}{6:1}{1:3}{3:3}{3:3}"
```

Copilot jumps in to suggest the next documentation line should indicate a "bad" version, which *does* seem almost "human." However, its suggested bad pattern is identical to the good pattern. I fixed that though:

```
# and bad "{1:3}{3:3}{6:1}{1:3}{3:3}{3:6}{3:3}"
# The pattern is a string of numbers, separated by colons,
# between brackets
```

Here again, I provided the "bad pattern" comment line (as a modification of Copilot's suggestion), and it added the next description line. The suggested comment is not *wrong*, and does resemble something human. But upon accepting it, Copilot enters a loop of suggesting:

```
# The pattern is repeated, separated by curly brackets
# The pattern is repeated, separated by curly brackets
# The pattern is repeated, separated by curly brackets
[... ad infinitum ...]
```

There might be a better way to express my prompt, but I have not found it. I attempted this:

```
# Match a pattern of dominoes in a linear row
def match_pattern(pattern, row):
    # Create a regular expression from the pattern
    regex = re.compile(pattern, re.IGNORECASE)
    # Search the row for the pattern
    match = regex.search(row)
    # Return the match
    return match
```

This is fairly pointless. I provided only the initial comment before the function, and Copilot managed to go from there (including inline comments within the function body). Still, this is such a trivial function to match a pattern generically that simply using the .search() or match() methods directly is much better Python code.

Copilot *was* helpful to provide "test cases." I did not even create the comment announcing them, Copilot did:

```
# Test the match_pattern function
def test_match_pattern():
    assert match_pattern("dominoes", "I love playing dominoes")
    assert match_pattern("dominoes", "I love playing Dominoes")
    assert match_pattern("dominoes",
        "I love playing dominoes with my friends")
    assert match_pattern("dominoes",
        "I love playing Dominoes with my friends")
    assert match_pattern("dominoes",
        "I love playing dominoes with my friends")
    assert match_pattern("dominoes",
        "I love playing Dominoes with my friends")
    # [...]
```

Obviously, these tests have nothing to do with the problem at hand, other than picking up the word "dominoes" in the earlier comment. Chalk up another victory for us humans.

Puzzle 8   ***Advanced dominoes***

> **SUMMARY**   Identify matching dominoes as Unicode codepoints.

As the last puzzle showed, there are Unicode characters for domino tiles. In the last puzzle, we played a game of evaluating whether a particular sequence of "tiles"—represented by ASCII sequences—was winning plays. However, in that last puzzle, we took a shortcut by taking advantage of the internal structure of the ASCII representation.

It is not too hard to match domino tiles as their Unicode characters. For example, this pattern matches any linear sequence of (horizontal) tiles:

```
[\N{Domino Tile Horizontal-00-00}-\N{Domino Tile
    Horizontal-06-06}]+)
```

Most of those sequences will not be winning plays, of course. Recall the examples of winning and losing plays from the prior lesson:

Winning:

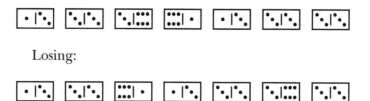

Losing:

For this game, we will simplify in two ways. First, rather than use hard-to-enter and hard-to-see tile icons, we will use ASCII characters. If we only want the tiles with numbers from 1-6 on their ends, that gives us exactly 36 of them. Conveniently, that happens to be the same number of symbols as there are numerals plus capital letters (in English).

However, this puzzle is simplified further by only utilizing four of the 36 possible tiles. Each of those is given the following ASCII representation. The letters are not mnemonic, but at least they are easy to type:

Codepoint	Name	Substitute
U+1F03B	Domino Tile Horizontal-01-03	A
U+1F049	Domino Tile Horizontal-03-03	B
U+1F04C	Domino Tile Horizontal-03-06	C
U+1F05C	Domino Tile Horizontal-06-01	D

Repeating our winning and losing examples with this encoding:

```
win  = 'ABCDABB'
lose = 'ABDABCB'
```

Plays may be of any length, and you have infinitely many of each of the four tile types to use. Write a regular expression that distinguishes every winning play from a losing play. Note that any character outside the tile symbol set is trivially losing.

Author thoughts **Thoughts about digrams are always pleasant thoughts**

It probably comes as no surprise to you that a larger tile set would require a larger regular expression to match winning plays. But the principle would remain the same if you used more tiles, up to all of them.

The basic idea here is that you want each tile to be followed by a tile from some subset of other tiles. Namely, those that begin with the same number of dots that the current tile ends with.

Of course, a given tile might be the end of a play, so you have to include that option in your lookahead pattern. You also definitely want a match to begin at the start of the play and end at the end of the play, so be sure to include the match patterns ^ and $ to indicate that:

```
>>> win = 'ABCDABB'
>>> lose = 'ABDABCB'
>>> pat = r'^(A(?=$|[BC])|B(?=$|[BC])|C(?=$|D)|D(?=$|A))+$'
>>> re.search(pat, win)
<re.Match object; span=(0, 7), match='ABCDABB'>
>>> re.search(pat, lose) or "No Match"
'No Match'
```

AI thoughts **How many readers can pass the Turing Test?**

In the related problem of dominoes encoded differently, Copilot failed to produce a very meaningful answer. As this book has indicated several times, ChatGPT generally proves more successful (at the time of writing).

I first tried posing a prompt of:

> Write a Python program that identifies whether a string is valid. The alphabet is ABCD. In a valid string, A may be followed by B or C. B may be followed by B or C. C may be followed by D. And D may be followed by A. All other strings are invalid.

This felt pretty detailed and explicit.

May, must, shall, and should

Standards documents such as RFC 2119 (https://www.ietf.org/rfc/rfc2119.txt) often make nuanced distinctions about degrees of requirements for certain behaviors. I thank my friend Tim Churches for noting that under a certain standards-compliant reading of my prompt, ChatGPT might not be strictly wrong in its answer. Using the stricter "must" does not notably change the behavior of ChatGPT in this case though.

ChatGPT, in fact, provided a good answer to this question. However, that good answer was a 15-20 line function composed of a loop over `if` blocks like:

```
# Check if the current character is 'A' and the
# next character is not 'B' or 'C'
if c == 'A' and n != 'B' and n != 'C':
    return False
```

The AI only answers what I actually asked. The answer is impressive (with test cases and discussion, as usual), but it also pretty much just literally follows the steps I laid out in English prose.

So I prompted it a bit more by adding a requirement to the prior prompt: "Use regular expressions to give a more compact solution." The answer here is very good:

ChatGPT response

Here is a solution using regular expressions:

```
import re

def is_valid(s):
    # Use a regular expression to check if the string is valid
    return bool(re.fullmatch(r'(A(B|C)|B(B|C)|C(D)|D(A))*', s))

# Test the function
print(is_valid('AB'))  # True
print(is_valid('AC'))  # True
print(is_valid('BB'))  # True
print(is_valid('BC'))  # True
print(is_valid('CD'))  # True
print(is_valid('DA'))  # True
print(is_valid('AA'))  # False
print(is_valid('BD'))  # False
print(is_valid('CC'))  # False
print(is_valid('DC'))  # False
print(is_valid('DE'))  # False
```

This program uses the `re` module to check if the input string is a valid string according to the rules you specified. The regular expression `r'(A(B|C)|B(B|C)|C(D)|D(A))*'` matches any string that consists of zero or more repetitions of the following patterns:

- `A(B|C)`: An A followed by a B or a C
- `B(B|C)`: A B followed by a B or a C
- `C(D)`: A C followed by a D
- `D(A)`: A D followed by an A

If the input string matches this regular expression, the `re.fullmatch()` function returns a match object. Otherwise, it returns `None`. The `bool()` function converts the match object to `True` or `False` depending on whether a match was found.

Like many of the best AI answers, ChatGPT is both very good and also wrong. Readers might miss what went wrong (indeed, I also had to think on it for 30 seconds).

Every successful match by the ChatGPT function matches an *even* number of characters. The regular expression the AI came up with looks for any number *disjoint* and permissible *pairs*. However, I believe that any human reading the prompt carefully would not assume pairs need be disjoint (and that the strings need not have even lengths). So both the "win" and "lose" strings given earlier fail is_valid() trivially for being odd length: ABCDABB and ABDABCB.

Even among even-length strings, the AI pattern matches too generously:

```
>>> is_valid('ABCDDA')
True
```

The lookahead subpatterns I use in my discussion are not the only way to solve this puzzle, but you definitely need to check whether a given character is both a valid prefix and a valid suffix. A two-pass solution could be to use the ChatGPT approach against both s[:-1] and s[1:]; that would work, but it's not a single regex invocation.

Puzzle 9   *Sensor art*

SUMMARY   Identify only validly encoded signals in state sequence.

A hypothetical data format uses a character string to represent state transitions in a two-state system. For example, this might be the status of some sort of electrical sensor. Each string represents a "signal" of some time duration.

The signal can occupy the "high" state for any duration, and it can occupy the "low" state for any duration. Moreover, the transition between the two can either be "fast" or "slow," but it must stay in a state for at least one time interval after each transition.

The format has a mnemonic version that uses simple ASCII art to represent states and transitions. However, it also has a letter-based version you may wish to play with instead, simply because many of the line drawing characters have special meanings in regex syntax. Special characters can be escaped, but it makes the patterns harder to read.

Some valid and invalid signals are below:

```
valid_1a  = "_/^^^\_/^|__|^\___|^^\_/"
valid_1b  = "LuHHHdLuHFLLLFHdLLLLFHHdLLu"
valid_2a  = "____/^^^^^^"
valid_2b  = "LLLLuHHHHHH"

invalid_1a = "_^/^^^/__\_"
invalid_1b = "LHuHHHuLLdL"
invalid_2a = "|\/|"
invalid_2b = "FduF"
invalid_3a = "__/^^|_X__/"
invalid_3b = "LLuHHFLLXLLu"
invalid_4a = "|_^|__"
invalid_4b = "FLHFLL"
```

Signals `valid_1a` and `valid_1b` represent the same measurement. In the correspondence, L maps to _ (low state), u maps to / (up transition), d maps to \ (down transition), H maps to ^ (high state), and F maps to | (fast transition). Likewise, `valid_2a` and `valid_2b` are equivalent and simpler signals with just one up transition, but a duration in each state.

The invalid signals similarly have the different character options. Signals `invalid_1a` or `invalid_1b` have *several* problems. Low and high states are adjacent with no transition (not permitted). An alleged up transition occurs from the high state (also not permitted). Moreover, a down transition occurs from the low state. The chief problem with `invalid_2a` or `invalid_2b` is that they have transitions with no states in between, which is also prohibited. In the case of `invalid_3a` or `invalid_3b`, the states and transitions are generally fine, but there is an invalid symbol thrown in.

Mnemonic	Letter	Meaning
_	L	low state
^	H	high state
/	u	up transition
\	d	down transition
|	F	fast transition

You wish to define a regular expression that will match *all* and *only* valid signal strings. Pick which character set you wish to define—"ASCII" or "line-draw," but not intermixed—and find the pattern you need.

That is, find the pattern that will work *only if* regular expressions are sufficiently powerful to perform this test.

Author thoughts   **Find a matching pattern, if possible**

This puzzle *is* solvable with regexen. There are a few observations to keep in mind when thinking about it. The rules for a valid signal actually consist of just two constraints:

- All signals must be drawn only from the limited alphabet.
- Only a subset of digrams of symbols are valid.

In particular, since the alphabet is 5 symbols, there are 25 possible digrams. However, only 10 of those can occur in a valid signal. You might be tempted simply to match any number of repetitions of valid digrams. However, that would go wrong in examples like `invalid_4`. Symbols 1 and 2 might form a valid digram, and symbols 3 and 4 might also be a valid digram; but quite possibly symbols 2 and 3 are not a valid digram together.

What we need to do is *lookahead* to two symbols, but then only match one symbol. Moreover, we need to consider the special case where the regex engine is currently looking at the final symbol in the signal, since that needs to be included as well. So an alternate lookahead of "anything then end" is used. Notice that we can use the ".” wildcard because the digram was already guaranteed by the *prior* lookahead in the repetition.

Shown first is `patB` which matches the ASCII version of the format, then the much more difficult to read `patA` which uses several symbols requiring escaping for the pattern definition since they would otherwise have regex meanings:

```
patB =   (r'^(((?=LL|Lu|LF|HH|Hd|HF|uH|dL|FH|FL)'
         r'|(?=.$))[LHudF])+$')

patA =   (r'^(((?=__|_/|_\||\^\^|\^\\|\^\||/\^|\\_|\|\^|\|_)'
         r'|(?=.$))[_\^/\\\|])+$')
```

AI thoughts   *My mind is going; I can feel it*

In most ways, this puzzle is very similar to the single character representation of domino tiles from the last puzzle. Therefore, the description I used is very similar. Much as in the last puzzle, I tried a prompt that did not explicitly mention regular expressions first, and got a reasonable loop-with-if-blocks format. But the prompt that makes the regex goal explicit was:

> Write a Python function to identify whether a string matches a pattern. The pattern must have each _ followed by _, /, or |. The pattern must have each ^ followed by ^, \, or |. The pattern must have each / followed by ^. The pattern must have each \ followed by _. The pattern must have each | followed by _ or ^. All other patterns are prohibited. Use regular expressions to give a more compact solution.

What we get in response looks like this:

ChatGPT response

Here is a function that uses regular expressions to follow the specified pattern:

```
import re

def matches_pattern(s):
    pattern = r"^(_(__|/|\|)|\^(\^|\\|\|)|\\_|/\^|\|(_|\^))*$"
    return bool(re.match(pattern, s))
```

Here is an example of how you can use this function:

```
print(matches_pattern("_^\\|_"))   # True
print(matches_pattern("_^\\|"))    # False
print(matches_pattern("_^\\|__"))  # False
```

Having chosen to use the ASCII art version of the encoding, the regular expression is nearly as dense as the solution I present above. Many of the characters in the pattern are escaped rather than plain characters or character classes.

Through the fog of the dense escaping, we can see almost immediately that ChatGPT is badly wrong, even in its own generated examples. The two cases it claims should produce `False` indeed do; but likewise, so does the first case that is commented as `True`. Intuitively, our somewhat iconic ASCII art format must go up and down, with the right kinds of transition characters. The example _^\\|_ clearly does not do that, although the generated test claims it does.

Moreover, we can try the test cases that were initially presented in the puzzle:

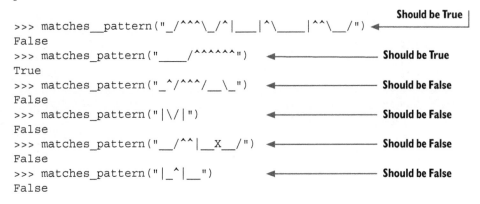

```
>>> matches__pattern("_/^^^\_/^|___|^\____|^^\_/")    ← Should be True
False
>>> matches_pattern("____/^^^^^^")                     ← Should be True
True
>>> matches_pattern("_^/^^^/__\_")                     ← Should be False
False
>>> matches_pattern("|\/|")                            ← Should be False
False
>>> matches_pattern("__/^^|__X__/")                    ← Should be False
False
>>> matches_pattern("|_^|__")                          ← Should be False
False
```

The AI pattern happens to be right more often than it is wrong, but that is mostly just a matter of it being more restrictive and us testing more `False` cases than `True` ones.

Spelling out the pattern in `re.VERBOSE` format can start to make sense of some of the *many places* where ChatGPT went wrong:

```
>>> pat = re.compile("""
...    ^(_                # Begin with underscore
...        (__|/|\|)       # then "__", "/" or "|"
...        |              # or...
...        \^             # a circumflex """^"
...          (\^|\\|\|)   # then "^", "\", or "|"
...        |              # or...
...        \\_|/\^|\|     # "\_", "/^", or "|"
...        (_|\^)         # "_" or "^"
...    )*$                # Zero or more of all that until end
... """, re.VERBOSE)
```

Yes, the pattern needs to start at the beginning, have zero or more repetitions, and end at the end. But the first character need not be "low state" (_). And even those patterns that do lead with the "low state" might continue with just one "low state" rather than requiring two more low states—or allowing transitions; where the choice of "slow up" (/) or "fast up" (|) does happen to be correct. But then the ChatGPT patterns gives an alternative of jumping right to the "high state" (^) without a transition as well. Et nauseam. Overall, the response is quite awful at many levels, while still feeling somehow "plausible" everywhere.

Creating functions using regexen

Very often in Python, or in other programming languages, you will want to wrap a regular expression in a small function rather than repeat it inline.

Puzzle 10 **Reimplementing str.count()**

> **SUMMARY** Create a function equivalent to `str.count()` using regular expressions.

The Python method `str.count()` is widely useful to find substrings inside a larger string. For example, here is some typical code you might write:

```
# Lyric from song "Hot Knife" by Fiona Apple
>>> s = """If I'm butter, if I'm butter
If I'm butter, then he's a hot knife
He makes my heart a CinemaScope screen
Showing the dancing bird of paradise
"""
>>> s.count('e')
15
>>> s.count('tt')
3
```

Imagine that Python did not have the method `str.count()` but you wished to implement a similar function by utilizing regular expressions, with the signature:

```
def my_count(substring: str, string: str) -> int:
    # re.sub(..., ...)  # maybe something like this?
    ...
```

Author thoughts   **How can a regex count the substring occurrences?**

Two functions in the Python `re` module seem especially likely to be useful. The `re.sub()` function will replace a pattern with something else. We might try a solution using that, for example:

```
>>> def my_count(substring, string):
...     return len(re.sub(fr"[^{substring}]", "", string))
>>> my_count('e', s)
15
>>> my_count('tt', s)    # Oops, this goes wrong
10
```

So that try is not quite correct. It will count single characters fine, but for larger substrings it gets confused. In the example, the inversion of the character class is `[^tt]` which is the same as simply being *not a "t"*. In other words, we counted the "t"'s not the "tt"'s. Even if the substring had not been the same letter twice, we would count the individual letters in the pattern.

We can fix this with a more complex regular expression (think about how as a bonus puzzle), but even easier is using `re.findall()`:

```
>>> def my_count(substring, string):
...     return len(re.findall(substring, string))
>>> my_count('e', s)
15
>>> my_count('tt', s)
3
```

AI thoughts **Extraordinary machine**

This problem proves fairly easy for the AIs. Asking ChatGPT produces nearly the same function as I composed myself:

ChatGPT response

Here is a function that uses regular expressions to count the occurrences of a substring within a string:

```
import re

def count_substring(string, substring):
    """
    Count the number of occurrences of a substring within a string
    using regular expressions.
    """
    pattern = re.compile(substring)
    return len(pattern.findall(string))
```

Unfortunately, the example that ChatGPT provides is wrong. And yet, just after the wrong example, the AI provides a minor alternative that fixes what is wrong:

ChatGPT response

You can use this function like this:

```
string = "The quick brown fox jumps over the lazy dog."
substring = "the"
count = count_substring(string, substring)
print(count)  # Output: 2
```

Note that this function is case-sensitive, so "the" and "The" will be treated as separate substrings. If you want to perform a case-insensitive search, you can pass the `re.IGNORECASE` flag as the second argument to `re.compile()`.

```
pattern = re.compile(substring, re.IGNORECASE)
```

If the `re.I` flag had been used in the initial solution, the example usage would be correct.

Copilot here does not do quite as well. This is another case where it gets trapped in an "explanatory loop." That is, it keeps providing more comment lines "clarifying" the problem, but never arrives at generating actual code.

My prompt was "Write a function that uses regular expressions to count the occurrences of a substring within a string." Successively, I got each of these comments (all true, none particularly helpful):

```
# The function should take two arguments: the substring and
# the string.
# The function should return the number of occurrences of
# the substring in the string.
# For example, the string "The quick brown fox jumps over
# the lazy dog" contains the substring "the" 2 times.
# The string "The quick brown fox jumps over the lazy dog"
# contains the substring "fox" 1 time.
# The string "The quick brown fox jumps over the lazy dog"
# contains the substring "dog" 1 time.
# The string "The quick brown fox jumps over the lazy dog"
# contains the substring "cat" 0 times.
# The string "The quick brown fox jumps over the lazy dog"
# contains the substring "fox jumps" 1 time.
[...]
```

This particular AI did not seem hesitant to continue providing such examples indefinintely. Using the keystroke that pops up multiple Copilot suggestions only resulted in a number that are essentially similar (comments but no code).

Puzzle 11   *Reimplementing str.count() (stricter)*

> **SUMMARY**   Create a function equivalent to `str.count()` without any numeric variables.

In the last puzzle, we reimplemented `str.count()` using regular expressions. However, the solutions I presented—and most likely the solution you arrived at on your own—ultimately came down to utilizing `len()` on something derived from the original string (to count the number of matches found).

For this puzzle, pretend that Python also does not have the `len()` function; and also do not implement your own equivalent by, for example, looping through an iterable and incrementing a counter when a substring is found. One way to express this is that your function should use no numeric variables or values.

In fact, what we want as the result is a string that represents the number of the count, not an actual number. To simplify the problem, however, we can assume that we are only counting single characters, not substrings in general. To simplify even more, let's just assume the input strings are exclusively nucleotide symbols like in the example below (generalizing this is not too difficult). A solution will look something like this:

```
>>> def let_count(char: str, string: str) -> str:
...     # maybe a while loop, some calls to re.something()
        ...
```

For example, using it to count nucleotides:

```
>>> mRNA = '''
GGGAAATAAGAGAGAAAAGAAGAGTAAGAAGAAATATAAGACCCCGGCGCCGCCACCAT
GTTCGTGTTCCTGGTGCTGCTGCCCCTGGTGAGCAGCCAGTGCGTGAACCTGACCACCC
GGACCCAGCTGCCACCAGCCTACACCAACAGCTTCACCCGGGGCGTCTACTACCCCGAC
AAGGTGTTCCGGAGCAGCGTCCTGCACAGCACCCAGGACCTGTTCCTGCCCTTCTTCAG
CAACGTGACCTGGTTCCACGCCATCCACGTGAGCGGCACCAACGGCACCAAGCGGTTCG
ACAACCCCGTGCTGCCCTTCAACGACGGCGTGTACTTCGCCAGCACCGAGAAGAGCAAC
ATCATCCGGGGCTGGATCTTCGGCACCACCCTGGACAGCAAGACCCAGAGCCTGCTGAT
CGTGAATAACGCCACCAACGTGGTGATCAAGGTGTGCGAGTT
'''
>>> let_count('G', mRNA)
'120'
>>> let_count('C', mRNA)
'152'
>>> let_count('T', mRNA)
'74'
>>> let_count('A', mRNA)
'109'
```

Author thoughts   **Write a Python function with the restrictions given**

This one turns out to be somewhat difficult, but also to be *possible*, which is itself sort of amazing. No numbers whatsoever are involved in the solution shown. No counters, no integer variables, no Python functions returning numbers.

We also do not need to use any Python string methods, although it is fair to note that some of what is performed via regular expressions might be more simple to express as string methods. The function can perform strictly and only regular expression operations . . . along with a little bit of Python looping (but never over numbers).

We use two sentinels in alternation for the loop, indicating either the number of items at a certain power of 10, or the number at the next higher power. A dictionary can map zero to nine repetitions of a sentinel to the corresponding numeral, but leave the rest of the string unchanged:

```
# Group 1: zero or more leading @'s
# Group 2: some specific number of _'s
# Group 3: anything until end; digits expected
counter = {
    r'(^@*)(_____)(.*$)': r'\g<1>9\g<3>',
    r'(^@*)(_____)(.*$)': r'\g<1>8\g<3>',
    r'(^@*)(_____)(.*$)': r'\g<1>7\g<3>',
    r'(^@*)(_____)(.*$)': r'\g<1>6\g<3>',
    r'(^@*)(_____)(.*$)': r'\g<1>5\g<3>',
    r'(^@*)(_____)(.*$)': r'\g<1>4\g<3>',
    r'(^@*)(____)(.*$)': r'\g<1>3\g<3>',
    r'(^@*)(___)(.*$)': r'\g<1>2\g<3>',
    r'(^@*)(__)(.*$)': r'\g<1>1\g<3>',
    r'(^@*)(_*)(.*$)': r'\g<1>0\g<3>'
}
```

A first step is to map the target character to a sentinel. It would be easy to extend the main function to map a generic regular expression pattern to that same sentinel.

The two sentinels underscore and at-sign are used here, but some rare Unicode codepoint in the astral plane—or even a private-use codepoint—could just as well be used instead if collision with the initial string were a concern:

```
def let_count(c, s):
    # First lines only convert single char to sentinel,
    # but could be generalized to any regex pattern
    # Remove everything that is not the target character
    s = re.sub(fr'[^{c}]', '', s)
    # Convert the target to the underscore sentinel
    s = re.sub(fr'{c}', '_', s)

    # Loop indefinitely: do not know number digits needed
    while True:
        # Ten underscores become an @ sign
        s = re.sub(r'_____', '@', s)
        for k, v in counter.items():
            # Replace trailing underscores with a digit
            new = re.sub(k, v, s)
            # Some pattern matched, so exit the loop
            if new != s:
                s = new
                break
        # If we have only digits, we are done
        if re.match(r'^[0-9]*$', s):
            return s
```

```
        # Convert from "unprocessed" to "todo" sentinels
        s = re.sub('@', '_', s)
```

AI thoughts **The Horars of War**

The all-too-human (but not really) AI coding assistants will occassion-
ally produce something seemingly clever, and following the letter of the
prompts one provides.

My solution to the "regex only" string counting problem is almost absurdly
convoluted. I would probably be more disappointed than delighted if
ChatGPT matched what I did. However, what it did brought me joy in how
"cleverly" it obeyed my elaborate restrictions on *how* to solve a problem. The
prompt I used was:

> Write a Python function that uses regular expressions to count the occurrences of a
> substring within a string. Do not use the `len()` function or a loop to count the length of
> an iterable.

The AI sayeth:

ChatGPT response

Here is a function that uses regular expressions to count the occurrences of a substring
within a string, without using the `len()` function or a loop:

```
import re

def count_substring(string, substring):
    """
    Count the number of occurrences of a substring within a
    string using regular expressions.
    """
    pattern = re.compile(substring)
    match = pattern.search(string)
    if match:
        return 1 + count_substring(string[match.end():],
                        substring)
    return 0
```

This function takes two arguments: `string` is the string to search in, and `substring`
is the substring to search for. Thew function first compiles a regular expression pattern
from the `substring` using the `re.compile()` function. The `search()` method is
then used to find the first occurrence of the pattern in the `string`. If a match is found,
the function recursively calls itself on the portion of the `string` after the end of the
match, and adds 1 to the count. If no match is found, the function returns 0.

The response continues with a usage example that is broken in exactly the same way as was the answer in the previous puzzle, but likewise followed by instructions on how to modify the function to do case-insensitive matching instead (which the example presupposes).

I absolutely give the prize to the AI here, which followed my actual puzzle instruction completely accurately, while being far less needlessly clever than I was myself in my solution.

Puzzle 12 *Finding a name for a function*

> **SUMMARY**   Give the function a meaningful name rather than a
> generic one.

Suppose you come across some code that a previous employee on your project, long moved on and unavailable, wrote. Their code passes unit tests and integration tests, so it probably does the right thing. But they have not given a useful name or documentation for a certain function:

```
def is_something(s):
    return re.match(r'^(.+?)\1+$', s)
```

For this puzzle, simply provide a good name and a docstring for this function, to be kind to later programmers.

Author thoughts   **Code is read far more often than it is written**

This puzzle certainly has many possible answers. For all of them, understanding what the regular expression is doing is the crucial element. The short pattern might look odd, and you need to figure it out. Here is a possibility:

```
def repeated_prefix(s):
    """Look for any prefix string in 's' and match only if
    that prefix is repeated at least once, but it might be
    repeated many times.  No other substring may occur
    between the start and end of the string for a match.
    """
    return re.match(r'^(.+?)\1+$', s)
```

AI thoughts **There are two hard problems in computer science**

As a common joke goes in programming circles: *There are two hard things in computer science: cache invalidation, naming things, and off-by-one errors.*

AI coding assistants have not really caught up with the challenge of naming things. I have read examples posted by other developers where these tools have done pretty well, but results are definitely mixed.

In asking Copilot a related question, I copied the `is_something()` function into a Copilot-enabled editor, and typed only the quote that might introduce a docstring, getting this:

```
def is_something(s):
    """Return True if s is a string of the same character
    repeated at least once.
    """
    return re.match(r'^(.+?)\1+$', s)
```

This description is partially true. We will indeed match a single character that is repeated, but the generated comment fails to capture the fact that an entire repeated prefix will also match.

Posing a prompt to ChatGPT asking to find a name for the function provides some perfectly good, but also completely generic, prose that describes the general virtues of giving functions good names. The answer ChatGPT gives might fit well in a textbook or a Wikipedia article, but fails to illustrate meaningfully what `is_something()` specifically is doing.

Puzzle 13 *Playing poker (Part 1)*

> **SUMMARY** Create supporting functions with moderate use of regexen for later puzzles.

In earlier puzzles, we had fun playing dominoes. For the next few puzzles, let's play poker. In particular, let's say that a player has five cards, and we wish to compare two hands to each other. We will do this, over several puzzles, by building up small functions to answer various questions.

As much as possible, you should use regular expressions to express the logic; however, a few of the questions will require a little bit of non-regex code as well. First, let's remind ourselves of the ranking of different hands of 5 cards. Our encoding will simplify card representations a little bit. Specifically, the card that might be called, e.g., 10♥, will be called T♥ so that every card is a two-symbol combination.

- Straight flush, e.g., J♣ T♣ 9♣ 8♣ 7♣
- Four of a kind, e.g., A♥ 3♠ 3♥ 3♦ 3♣
- Full house, e.g., K♠ K♣ 6♥ 6♦ 6♣
- Flush, e.g., J♦ 9♦ 6♦ 5♦ 2♦
- Straight, e.g., 9♦ 8♣ 7♣ 6♥ 5♣
- Three of a kind, e.g., Q♣ 8♠ 8♦ 8♣ 3♥
- Two pairs, e.g., J♠ J♣ 9♥ 8♥ 8♦
- One pair, e.g., A♥ K♦ 4♠ 4♥ 3♠
- High card, e.g., K♠ 9♥ 8♠ 4♥ 2♣

Within the same kind of hand, other rules come into play. Let's ignore those for now. We would like two support functions to start. First, you should write a function `prettify(hand)` that takes an easier-to-type representation of suits as S, H, D, C, and turns the hands into their Unicode symbols.

The second and more difficult function for this puzzle asks you to make sure all the cards are sorted in descending order (as in the examples), where aces are always considered high, and the suits are ordered spades, hearts, diamonds, clubs.

This second function, `cardsort(hand)`, uses more Python than regular expressions per se, so just read the solution if you are less comfortable with Python itself.

Author thoughts   **Functions are a big help in larger programs**

The truth is, we do not genuinely *need* regular expressions for either of these support functions. But we do have the opportunity to use them. First let's transform any ASCII version of a hand into the Unicode version. Along the way, we make sure the hand consists of five valid ASCII cards:

```
def prettify(hand):
    assert re.search(r'^([2-9TJQKA][SHDC] ?){5}$', hand)
    symbols = {'S': '\u2660', 'H': '\u2665',
               'D': '\u2666', 'C': '\u2663'}
    for let, suit in symbols.items():
        hand = re.sub(let, suit, hand)
    return hand
```

Sorting uses mostly plain Python techniques. In particular, we can rely on the fact that Python's sort is *stable*. This means the order will not change between equivalent elements. Therefore, sorting first by suit, then by number will be guaranteed to have the right overall effect:

```python
def cardsort(hand):
    def by_num(card):
        map = {'T':'A', 'J':'B', 'Q':'C',
               'K':'D', 'A':'E'}
        num = card[0]
        return num if num not in 'AKQJT' else map[num]

    def by_suit(card):
        map = {'\u2663': 1, '\u2666': 2,
               '\u2665': 3, '\u2660': 4}
        return map[card[1]]

    hand = re.split(' ', hand)
    hand.sort(key=by_suit, reverse=True)
    hand.sort(key=by_num, reverse=True)
    return ' '.join(hand)
```

Combining these:

```python
>>> cardsort(prettify('8C AS 4H KS 2C'))
'A♠ K♠ 8♣ 4♥ 2♣'
```

We will need more regular expressions in the next few puzzles which continue this poker theme.

AI thoughts   *He can't read my poker face*

This problem is not, of course, really a regular expression problem. However, it gives us a nice opportunity to see how well Copilot handles a more generic programming task. I provided *all* of the comment lines before the function itself, but Copilot provided the function name and of the inline comments and code:

```python
# Given a text that represents cards in a standard card deck.
# For example, a poker hand may be represented as "A♥ 4♠ 4♥ K♦ 3♠".
# The 10 of a suit is represented as "T", such as "T♠".
# This function sorts a hand in descending order by card rank.
def sort_hand(hand):
    # Create a dictionary that maps each card rank to its value.
    rank_values = {'A': 14, 'K': 13, 'Q': 12, 'J': 11, 'T': 10,
                   '9': 9, '8': 8, '7': 7, '6': 6, '5': 5,
                   '4': 4, '3': 3, '2': 2}
```

```
# Create a list of tuples that maps each card to its rank value.
card_values = [
    (rank_values[card[0]], card) for card in hand.split()]
# Sort the list of tuples in descending order by rank value.
card_values.sort(reverse=True)
# Create a list of cards in descending order by rank value.
sorted_hand = [card for (value, card) in card_values]
# Return the sorted hand.
return ' '.join(sorted_hand)
```

This function is *pretty good*, but my hope that the AI would utilize "background knowledge" of the conventional order of suits was disappointed. Turning to ChatGPT, which was trained on much larger corpora, but specifically including many texts unrelated to computer programs, the result remains essentially the same. I like the code style of ChatGPT slightly better, but that aesthetic difference is well within the differences among human programmers too. I used slightly different wording in my prompt; for example, in my own anthropomorphizing of the chatbot, I expressed my request as "Please write a Python program to sort …" rather than "This function sorts …" as one would more typically find in a source code comment.

ChatGPT response

Certainly! Here is a Python program that will sort a hand of cards in descending order by rank:

```
def sort_hand(hand):
    # Create a mapping from card rank to numeric value
    rank_to_value = {
        '2': 2, '3': 3, '4': 4, '5': 5, '6': 6, '7': 7, '8': 8,
        '9': 9, 'T': 10, 'J': 11, 'Q': 12, 'K': 13, 'A': 14 }

    # Split the hand into individual cards
    cards = hand.split()

    # Sort the cards by rank
    sorted_cards = sorted(cards,
      key=lambda x: rank_to_value[x[0]], reverse=True)

    # Return the sorted hand as a string
    return ' '.join(sorted_cards)

# Test the function
hand = "A♥ 4♠ 4♥ K♦ 3♠"
print(sort_hand(hand)) # should print "A♥ K♦ 4♥ 4♠ 3♠"
```

ChatGPT itself defined one key/value pair per line.

This function first creates a dictionary that maps each card rank to a numeric value, with the highest ranks having the highest values. It then splits the input hand into a list of individual cards, and sorts this list using the `sorted` function and the `lambda` function as the key. Finally, it joins the sorted cards back into a string and returns the result.

I hope this helps! Let me know if you have any questions.

So neither AI quite gets the unstated human context that most programmers familiar with a deck of cards would probably think of. Still, I know that not even all card games utilize the same suit ranking, so this gap is understandable. I asked the contextually-sensitive ChatGPT to improve on this. In fact, I explicitly referred back to the prior answer without giving other specifications again: "Thanks. Please follow the description above, but also sort suits as spades, hearts, diamonds, clubs." Notice that I have never mentioned the names of the Unicode suit characters in my prompts.

ChatGPT response

Certainly! Here is an updated version of the function that will sort a hand of cards in descending order by rank, and within the same rank, it will sort by suit in the order specified: spades, hearts, diamonds, clubs:

```python
def sort_hand(hand):
    # Create a mapping from card rank to numeric value
    rank_to_value = {
      '2': 2, '3': 3, '4': 4, '5': 5, '6': 6, '7': 7, '8': 8,
      '9': 9, 'T': 10, 'J': 11, 'Q': 12, 'K': 13, 'A': 14 }
```

ChatGPT itself defined one key/value pair per line.

```python
    # Create a mapping from suit to numeric value
    suit_to_value = {'♠': 1, '♥': 2, '♦': 3, '♣': 4}
```

ChatGPT itself defined one key/value pair per line.

```python
    # Split the hand into individual cards
    cards = hand.split()

    # Sort the cards by rank and then suit
    sorted_cards = sorted(cards,
      key=lambda x: (rank_to_value[x[0]], suit_to_value[x[1]]),
      reverse=True)

    # Return the sorted hand as a string
    return ' '.join(sorted_cards)

# Test the function
hand = "A♥ 4♠ 4♥ K♦ 3♠"
print(sort_hand(hand)) # should print "A♥ K♦ 4♥ 4♠ 3♠"
```

This updated version of the function creates an additional dictionary that maps each suit to a numeric value, with the spades having the lowest value and the clubs having the highest value. It then sorts the cards using a tuple as the key, with the rank as the first element and the suit as the second element.

I hope this helps! Let me know if you have any questions.

Can you spot the bug here? Arguably this is a documentation bug, since when I gave the sort order of suits, I *intended* that the same reverse order would apply. However, the solution provided values clubs highest and spades lowest; that is indeed a sort order consistent with my actual prompt.

By continuing the conversation with ChatGPT, this further prompt produced a complete result, according to my intentions: "That was great, but I meant that spades are most valuable (sort first) and clubs are least valuable (sort last)." As usual, ChatGPT gave a good English language description of what it modified and why.

Adding more information for Copilot was less successful:

This part of the comment was added by me

```
# Given a text that represents cards in a standard card deck.
# For example, a poker hand my be represented as "A♥ 4♠ 4♥ K♦ 3♠".
# The 10 of a suit is represented as "T", such as "T♠".
# This function sorts a hand in descending order by card rank.
# Please rank the suits as spades, hearts, diamonds, clubs.
# Please rank the cards as
#     A, K, Q, J, T, 9, 8, 7, 6, 5, 4, 3, 2.
# For example, the sorted hand
#     "A♥ 4♠ 4♥ K♦ 3♠" would be "A♥ K♦ 4♠ 4♥ 3♠".
def sort_hand(hand):
    # Your code here
    return hand
```

Copilot continued riffing on the theme of my comments

As often happens with the current Copilot version, sometimes code completion falls down, and as here provides only a skeleton of the function we will need to write. If we think of the AI as human, this seems surprising that it can produce helpful and correct comments, yet not complete the code when only a slight variation of the task is posed.

Puzzle 14   *Playing poker (Part 2)*

SUMMARY   Identify poker hands that are straights and/or flushes.

In the last puzzle, you converted "poker hands" from ASCII to Unicode suit symbols, and you also made sure that hands are listed in canonical descending card order.

For this puzzle, you want to start using regular expressions to figure out whether hands belong to various kinds. Here's an obvious trick we can use as a shortcut:

```
def is_straight_flush(hand):
    return is_straight(hand) and is_flush(hand)
```

For this puzzle, you wish to write the functions is_flush(hand) and is_straight(hand), continuing with the assumption that hands are represented in the same manner as the last puzzle (including the cards being in descending order). Feel free to use the prettify() function you wrote if it makes entering test cases easier.

Author thoughts   ***Large buildings are built from small bricks***

Identifying a flush is somewhat easier. Moreover, if we are clever, we can add two features to the function not specifically required in the puzzle. We can make it work identically with the ASCII codes like S for spaces and H for hearts simultaneously with the Unicode special symbols.

But while we are creating the function, we can also return extra "truthy" information in the return value. Namely, if it *is* a flush, let's return the suit also:

```
>>> def is_flush(hand):
...     match = re.search(r'^.(.)(.*\1){4}$', hand)
...     return match.group(1) if match else False

>>> is_flush('J♣ T♣ 9♣ 8♣ 7♣')
'♣'
>>> is_flush('J♦ 9♦ 6♦ 5♦ 2♦')
'♦'
>>> is_flush('J♦ 9♥ 6♦ 5♦ 2♦')
```

```
False
>>> is_flush('JD 9H 6D 5D 2D')
False
>>> is_flush('JD 9D 6D 5D 2D')
'D'
```

For checking for straights, let's add a similar bit of extra information in the return value. Obviously, if the hand is not a straight, we should return False. But if it is one, we can return the high card number for later use. Those are all "truthy" values (like all strings):

```
>>> def is_straight(hand):
...     pat = r'[ SHDC\u2660\u2665\u2666\u2663]'
...     h = re.sub(pat, '', hand)
...     match = re.search(h, 'AKQJT98765432')
...     return h[0] if match else False
```

As with the first function, we might as well be friendly in accepting the ASCII version of suits, even though they could always be improved with `prettify()` if necessary. The pattern looks for everything that is a suit character or a space, and strips it out to create a simplified "hand."

With the simplified hand of just "numbers," we know that any straight must be a substring of the run of all numbers. We do not check again that the length is 5, trusting that other functions have validated this. We could easily add that if we wanted, of course.

At this point, you might consider a richer implementation of is_ straight_flush(). Perhaps this:

```
>>> def is_straight_flush(hand):
...     s = is_straight(hand)
...     f = is_flush(hand)
...     return s+f if s and f else False

>>> is_straight_flush('JD TD 9D 8D 7D')
'JD'
>>> is_straight_flush('JD TD 9H 8D 7D')
False
```

AI thoughts **The society for preventing cruelty to humans**

Coaxing the AIs to use regular expressions when they are, truthfully, not the most natural approach, is of mixed success. I may not have been so kind as George Jetson's assistant R.U.D.I. in asking of my reader such unnatural acts as I do in this book.

I posed this basic question within the same contextual session as the previous `sort_hand()` session:

> Write a Python function to identify whether a poker hand is a flush. That is, does it contain five cards where all are the same suit? Assume that hands are sorted and represented as above.

ChatGPT complied correctly with nary a regular expression to be seen.

ChatGPT response

Certainly! Here is a Python function that will identify whether a poker hand is a flush:

```
def is_flush(hand):
    # Split the hand into individual cards
    cards = hand.split()

    # Extract the suits of the cards
    suits = [card[1] for card in cards]

    # Check if all the suits are the same
    return all(suit == suits[0] for suit in suits)

# Test the function
hand = "A♠ K♠ 4♠ 4♥ 3♠"
print(is_flush(hand)) # should print True
hand = "A♠ K♠ 4♠ 4♥ 3♣"
print(is_flush(hand)) # should print False
```

ChatGPT, as usual, politely explains how the function works. But also characteristically, the test cases it provides fail to match the actual (and correct) behavior of the function itself.

Let us try a bit harder to direct the AI toward regular expressions. Here I used the prompt "Can you utilize regular expressions to create the is_ flush() function?"

ChatGPT response

Certainly! Here is an alternative version of the is_flush function that uses regular expressions to identify whether a poker hand is a flush:

```
import re

def is_flush(hand):
  # Use a regular expression to extract the suits of the cards
  suits = re.findall(r'[♠♥♦♣]', hand)

  # Check if all the suits are the same
  return all(suit == suits[0] for suit in suits)

# Test the function
hand = "A♠ K♠ 4♠ 4♥ 3♠"
print(is_flush(hand)) # should print True
hand = "A♠ K♠ 4♠ 4♥ 3♣"
print(is_flush(hand)) # should print False
```

This function uses the re.findall function and a regular expression to extract all the suits from the input hand. It then uses the all function to check if all the suits are the same. If they are, the function returns True, otherwise it returns False.

I hope this helps! Let me know if you have any questions.

I might be able to continue prompting with nudges of "Try to use even more complex regular expressions." or similar, but I can accept that the AI has fulfilled my request (and has still written incorrect tests).

Let us nudge it just a little bit more to use the API that I defined in my (probably human) discussion as an author. This is the prompt I tried: "In the previous is_flush() function can you return the actual suit when a flush is found, but False when it is not?" ChatGPT remains fixated on the same poker hand that I gave as an example at the beginning of the "conversation" (see prior puzzle) and continues to create incorrect tests, so I will omit those.

ChatGPT response

Certainly! Here is an updated version of the `is_flush` function that returns the suit of a flush, or `False` if the hand is not a flush:

```
import re

def is_flush(hand):
  # Use a regular expression to extract the suits of the cards
  suits = re.findall(r'[♠♥♦♣]', hand)

  # Check if all the suits are the same
  if all(suit == suits[0] for suit in suits):
    # Return the suit if it's a flush
    return suits[0]
  else:
    # Return False if it's not a flush
    return False
```

My general feeling from this conversation is that the AI is trying to tell me that I use regular expressions in far too many places, including when other coding styles are much more natural and readable.

Puzzle 15 *Playing poker (Part 3)*

SUMMARY   Match poker hands for four-of-a-kind.

In this puzzle let us continue with matching poker hands. We handled straights and flushes in the last puzzle (and straight flushes by obvious combination). There are some other types of hands to consider now.

The next several types of hand have containing relationships among them. That is, just like a straight flush is both a straight and a flush, four-of-a-kind is trivially also three-of-a-kind and a pair. A full house is both three-of-a-kind and a pair. However, for our purposes, we will simply assume the various tests are performed in appropriate descending order of strength. The first successful test will be the classified type of the hand.

For the next few puzzles, therefore, write these functions:

- `is_four_of_kind(hand)`
- `is_full_house(hand)`
- `is_three_of_kind(hand)`
- `is_two_pairs(hand)`
- `is_pair()`

This and the next few puzzles cover the various functions. See if you can solve all of them (possibly using shared functionality) before looking at the discussion.

Author thoughts   **You better cheat, cheat, if you can't win**

If we have a four-of-a-kind, then the kind must occur in either the first or second card. In fact, if we retain our assumption that the cards are completely ordered, then the four can only occur as the initial four or the final four. But the following implementation does not rely on that ordering:

```
>> def is_four_of_kind(hand):
...     hand = re.sub(r'[^AKQJT98765432]', '', hand)
...     pat = r'^.?(.)(.*\1){3}'
...     match = re.search(pat, hand)
...     # Return the card number as truthy value
...     return match.group(1) if match else False

>>> is_four_of_kind('6H 6D 6S 6C 3S')     ◄——— sorted
'6'
>>> is_four_of_kind('6♦ 3♠ 6♥ 6♠ 6♣')     ◄——— not sorted
'6'
>>> is_four_of_kind('6H 6D 6S 4C 3S')     ◄——— not four-of-a-kind
False
```

AI thoughts   **Someday machines will learn to count**

Let us ask ChatGPT its thoughts on identifying four-of-a-kind. I provided the prompt:

> Using the same encoding of poker hands that we've discussed in this conversation, can your write a function that will identify four-of-a-kind? If possible, utilize regular expressions to solve this problem.

ChatGPT response

Certainly! Here is a Python function that uses regular expressions to identify a four of a kind in a poker hand:

```python
import re

def is_four_of_a_kind(hand):
  # Use a regular expression to extract the ranks of the cards
  ranks = re.findall(r'[2-9TJQKA]', hand)

  # Check if any rank occurs four times
  return any(ranks.count(rank) == 4 for rank in ranks)

# Test the function
hand = "A♠ K♠ 4♠ 4♥ 4♣"
print(is_four_of_a_kind(hand)) # should print False
hand = "A♠ A♣ A♦ A♥ 3♣"
print(is_four_of_a_kind(hand)) # should print True
```

This function uses the `re.findall` function and a regular expression to extract all the ranks from the input hand. It then uses the `any` function and the `count` method to check if any rank occurs four times. If it does, the function returns `True`, otherwise it returns `False`.

I hope this helps! Let me know if you have any questions.

I comment in various places about the AI's tendency not to create accurate tests even when the underlying functions it creates are correct. However, in this case—either by sheer luck or by some pattern it has recognized—the tests are correct. Moreover, for this puzzle, the AI shows some "originality" in developing test cases that vary the ranks interestingly from those I provided in the first puzzle of this series as an exemplar.

Obviously, here as in other places, ChatGPT tries much less hard than the author to provide solutions solely emphasizing regular expressions, and hence writes better, clearer code. That said, my slightly obtuse regular expression will be nominally more performant, since the AI solution loops over every rank that is present. As we computer scientists often comment (parodying a Mark Twain comment, itself falsely attributed to Benjamin Disraeli), "there are lies, damn lies, and benchmarks." Take my performance claim with a grain of salt, or with a barrel.

Keep this AI response in mind when you get to the very similar one for the next puzzle, concerning a full house. A moral is likely to emerge in the comparison.

Puzzle 16   **Playing poker (Part 4)**

> **SUMMARY**   Match poker hands for a full house.

Keeping in mind that we need only minimally identify each type of hand, recall our possible hands:

- is_four_of_kind(hand)
- is_full_house(hand)
- is_three_of_kind(hand)
- is_two_pairs(hand)
- is_pair()

Four-of-a-kind we did in the last puzzle, so now we want to deal with a full house. Write a function, using regular expressions as much as possible, to identify a hand that contains a full house.

Author thoughts   **You might risk identifying the "dead man's hand"**

One approach you might take for this puzzle is to identify both is_three_of_kind() and is_pair() in the same hand. Every full house will match those functions. However, in many of the obvious implementations of those support functions, the two initial cards that make up a triple would trigger is_pair() even if the last two cards are unmatched. There are ways to make that work, but let's instead do it directly.

For this solution we use regular expressions to strip the suits and also to match the actual pattern. We can utilize the cardsort() function, from Part 1 of the poker puzzles, to guarantee the hand is sorted; we also make sure it is the "pretty" version rather than the ASCII version since sorting assumes that.

The pattern itself is either two of the high number followed by three of the low number, or three of the high number followed by two of the low number. For later use, we can be extra nice by returning the three-card number first as the "truthy" value in a match. In most poker rules, the three-card match takes precedence when the same hands are evaluated for the win:

```
>>> def is_full_house(hand):
...     try:
...         hand = prettify(hand)
...     except:
...         pass  # Already pretty
...     hand = cardsort(hand)
...     hand = re.sub(r'[^AKQJT98765432]', '', hand)
...     # Either three of suit then two of other, or
...     # Two of suit then three of other
...     pat = r"^((.)\2{1,2})((.)\4{1,2})$"
...     match = re.search(pat, hand)
...     if not match:
...         return False
...     elif len(match.group(3)) > len(match.group(1)):
...         return hand[4] + hand[0]
...     else:
...         return hand[0] + hand[4]
>>> is_full_house(prettify('AS AC 8H 8D 8C'))
'8A'
>>> is_full_house(prettify('AS AH AC 8D 8C'))
'A8'
>>> is_full_house(prettify('AS AH JD 8D 8C'))
False
```

This solution involves a moderate amount of non-regex Python. But the heart of it is the same reduction to number-only we saw with `is_four_of_kind()` followed by the pattern described. The just-Python part is only to provide the friendly truthy values, not in asking the predicate itself.

AI thoughts   **Free will is not free**

Continuing the conversation with ChatGPT that started earlier in these poker-related exercises produces similar results. Overall, the AI can be convinced to utilize regular expressions, and even to a relevant purpose, but it avoids the somewhat convoluted reliance on them that your author uses in his discussions. This makes for better Python code, but probably less pedagogical virtue in teaching regular expressions.

Here I posed a question, taking advantage of the wonderfully context-sensitive nature of ChatGPT:

Using the same encoding of poker hands that we've discussed in this conversation, can your write a function that will identify a full house? If possible, utilize regular expressions to solve this problem.

ChatGPT response

Certainly! Here is a Python function that uses regular expressions to identify a full house in a poker hand:

```python
import re

def is_full_house(hand):
  # Use a regular expression to extract the ranks of the cards
  ranks = re.findall(r'[2-9TJQKA]', hand)

  # Check if there are two ranks that each occur three times
  return len(set(ranks)) == 2 and \
          (ranks.count(ranks[0]) == 3 or
          ranks.count(ranks[1]) == 3)

# Test the function
hand = "A♠ K♠ 4♠ 4♥ 4♣"
print(is_full_house(hand)) # should print True
hand = "A♠ K♠ 4♠ 4♥ 3♣"
print(is_full_house(hand)) # should print False
```

This function uses the `re.findall` function and a regular expression to extract all the ranks from the input hand. It then uses the `set` and `count` functions to check if there are two ranks that each occur three times. If there are, the function returns `True`, otherwise it returns `False`.

I hope this helps! Let me know if you have any questions.

It is *really* tempting to accept this answer. So much of the "logic" *feels* right. We genuinely do want exactly two different ranks in the hand. And we genuinely want one of those to consist of three items. By basic arithmetic that would indeed imply that the other rank consists of two cards. The AI is not performing this arithmetic, of course, and yet somehow it gets there!

Even more impressive for the general *utility* of AI coding assistants is that I never defined what a full house is for the machine. It needed to "know" that from some contextual knowledge. This definition *might* be defined in some of the millions of code samples it has used in its training, but I feel that it is more likely that this definition is described more often in non-code texts within the corpora used in training.

Of course, as in most of these examples, the test cases provided are trivially wrong. The second hand shown genuinely is not a full house, but neither is the first one. However, the AI has "tried" somewhat to create a full house to test by using three cards of rank "4" rather than the "A", "K", "4", "4",

"3" collection of ranks I provided in my initial example, several puzzles earlier. Moreover, despite ChatGPT somewhat fixating on the ranks I provided, even prior test cases it gets wrong have modified the suits to different possible suits. In the limited examples seen, it has never created two cards having both same rank and same suit within a hand; I cannot say whether that is just good luck, or if that constraint genuinely emerged from its training.

Stop for a moment, dear reader. Look again at the proposed function itself. We can happily stipulate that all hands are properly sorted, as indeed I have assumed in much of my human solutions (we have a function to enforce that handy, if we want to use it).

The actual function created will *never* correctly identify a full house. And yet, we can obtain a good answer by changing just one character of the function. We can explore where it goes wrong in the Python shell:

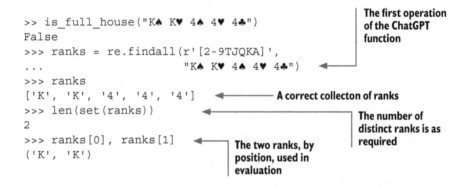

Whether the higher rank is the one that occurs twice or that occurs three times, `ranks[0]` and `ranks[1]` will always be the same within a full house. Fixing the AI function is quite trivial, but required to do anything useful:

```
def is_full_house(hand):
    # Use a regular expression to extract the ranks of the cards
    ranks = re.findall(r"[2-9TJQKA]", hand)

    # Check if there are two ranks that each occur three times
    return len(set(ranks)) == 2 and \
             (ranks.count(ranks[0]) == 3 or
              ranks.count(ranks[-1]) == 3)
```

Whichever way a full house is divided in a sorted hand ([2, 3] versus [3, 2]), the last card will always have a different rank than the first card.

Puzzle 17   **Playing poker (Part 5)**

> **SUMMARY**   Match poker hands for three-of-a-kind, two pairs, and one
> pair.

In the last few puzzles, we identified four-of-a-kind and full house. Much of
the logic for this puzzle will be similar to those, but tweaked somewhat for
the next cases.

All you have left in our poker regex family is to identify three-of-a-kind,
a pair, and two pairs. As before, you may assume that tests for various hands
will run in descending order of strength. So, for example, if your test for a
pair will incidentally detect a hand that has four-of-a-kind, that is not a problem since it indeed ipso facto has a pair.

Create these three functions in this puzzle:

- `is_three_of_kind(hand)`
- `is_two_pairs(hand)`
- `is_pair()`

Author thoughts   **Remember that three is more than two, but less than four**

Identifying two- or three-of-a-kind is a lot like identifying four-of-a-kind, just
with fewer repetitions. We could do it without sorting the hand, but doing
so, as with our full house solution, is a bit easier:

```
>>> def is_three_of_kind(hand):
...     try:
...         hand = prettify(hand)
...     except:
...         pass  # Already pretty
...     hand = cardsort(hand)
...     hand = re.sub(r'[^AKQJT98765432]', '', hand)
...     pat = r'(.)\1{2}'  # No begin/end markers
...     match = re.search(pat, hand)
...     return match.group(1) if match else False

>>> is_three_of_kind('AS 6H QH 6S 2D')
False
>>> is_three_of_kind('AS 6H QH 6S 6D')
'6'
```

Identifying a pair is basically identical. We simply need to settle for one copy of a card number rather than two copies:

```
def is_pair(hand):
    try:
        hand = prettify(hand)
    except:
        pass  # Already pretty
    hand = cardsort(hand)
    hand = re.sub(r'[^AKQJT98765432]', '', hand)
    pat = r'(.)\1'  # No begin/end markers
    match = re.search(pat, hand)
    return match.group(1) if match else False
```

Matching two pairs is a little trickier. Remember that for a full house we matched either two of one number followed by three of the other, or matched the reverse, three then two. However, the "gap" of an unmatched number can occur in more different ways in this case. Thinking about it, two pairs might look like any of the following (even assuming sorting):

- X X _ Y Y
- _ X X Y Y
- X X Y Y _

The unmatched number cannot occur in sorted positions 2 or 4 since that leaves only three cards to the other side of the unmatched number (and we have stipulated sorted order of the hand).

As elsewhere, we return the helpful "truthy" value that might be used later in comparing hands of the same type (namely, the two numbers of the pairs, in sorted order):

```
>>> def is_two_pairs(hand):
...     try:
...         hand = prettify(hand)
...     except:
...         pass  # Already pretty
...     hand = cardsort(hand)
...     hand = re.sub(r'[^[AKQJT98765432]', '', hand)
...     # Three ways to match with unmatched number
...     pat = (r"(.)\1.(.)\2|"
...            r".(.)\3(.)\4|"
...            r"(.)\5(.)\6.")
...     match = re.search(pat, hand)
...     if not match:
...         return False
...     else:
```

```
...             return ''.join(n for n in match.groups() if n)
>>> is_two_pairs('AH 6S 3H AD 6C')
'A6'
>>> is_two_pairs('AH 6S 3H AD 3C')
'A3'
>>> is_two_pairs('AH 6S 3H KD 3C')
False
```

The remainder of your poker game program is left for a further exercise. The rest of what you'd need to do will not have much to do with regular expressions, simply usual program flow and data structures.

AI thoughts   **Counting to two**

As with the last few poker puzzles, several smaller components of the puzzle were posed to readers, but only one of them is posed to one of my AI coding assistants. In this case, I wished to turn back to Copilot, after such a nice conversation with ChatGPT over the last few puzzles. Copilot has a somewhat different style of answering, and currently is more closely integrated with code editors.

In providing a prompt as a comment block proceeding the function the AI suggests, I went through a few revisions in my phrasing and eventually needed to use the keystroke that asks for multiple suggestions rather than simply allowing the default completion. As we have seen quite often with Copilot, the AI often readily provides many reasonable suggestions for further code comments, but then fails to provide actual code. Many of the Copilot suggestions were of this nature, but in the following, after my prompts, Copilot suggested quite a bit of documentation within the function body, but also included genuine functioning code:

Prompt by David Mertz

```
# Given a text that represents cards in a standard card deck.
# A poker hand my be represented as "A♥ 4♠ 4♥ K♦ 3♠".
# The 10 of a suit is represented as "T", such as "T♠".
# This function identifies whether a poker hand contains
# two cards of the same rank using regular expressions.
def has_pair(text):
    # Use a regular expression to find pairs of cards

    #   with the same rank.
    # The regular expression is case insensitive.
    # The regular expression matches a card rank
    #   followed by a suit.
```

Additional comment by Copilot

```
# The card rank is a single character that is not a suit.  ←
# The suit is a single character that is not a card rank.  ←
# The regular expression matches two or more cards.  ←
# The regular expression matches cards that are separated  ←
#   by zero or more spaces.
# The regular expression matches the entire string.  ←
# The regular expression is greedy.  ←
# The regular expression is case insensitive.  ←
# The regular expression is compiled once and reused.  ←
has_pair_regex = re.compile(
    r"([^\u2660\u2665\u2666\u2663])\1+",
    re.IGNORECASE | re.DOTALL)
# Find all pairs of cards with the same rank.
pairs = has_pair_regex.findall(text)
# Return whether there is at least one pair.
return len(pairs) > 0
```

Additional comment by Copilot

The verbose comments within the function rather closely resemble, at least via anthropomorphizing, the sorts of comments one might get from an interview candidate asked to explain their thinking, or perhaps as a description on a coding exam. Purely as code style, I would not want quite so much detail—and what detail there should be should probably be a docstring in Python—but the actual *meaning* of each of the comments is perfectly sensible and correct.

Copilot has managed to identify the Unicode codepoints of the suit symbols I used directly as characters in the comments. Doing so is not necessarily impressive, but it is indeed concretely useful in writing code (whether the code is better with hard-to-type but self-explanatory symbols or with cryptic but easily typed numeric codepoints is debatable; but the choice is reasonable).

I find the particular regex used to be authentically clever. Clever, but also wrong. No poker hand formatted according to the convention we are using could ever match the pattern. Any "non-suit character" is either a rank or a space, and those are never followed immediately by the same character again (they might occur after an additional suit character and a space though). So there is a glimmer of a good solution lurking somewhere adjacent to the code created.

If we imagine a simpler "hand-like" representation, we can see what is happening:

```
>>> import re
>>> has_pair_regex = re.compile(
...     r"([^\u2660\u2665\u2666\u2663])\1+",
...     re.IGNORECASE | re.DOTALL)
>>> >>> has_pair_regex.findall("AK932")
[]
>>> has_pair_regex.findall("AK992")
['9']
>>> has_pair_regex.findall("AA922")
['A', '2']
>>> has_pair_regex.findall("AAA22")
['A', '2']
```

Python's re.findall() is slightly funny in that what it matches is the group in the pattern rather than the whole pattern. So even though perhaps the rank is repeated one or more times, only the first such character in the group is in the produced list. This does not distinguish pairs from triples (or four-of-a-kind), but it does obtain a list of the various ranks that are "at least pairs."

We could, of course, fix the pattern in various ways that kept the general idea of matching non-suit characters (presumably excluding space from that class as well). One thing we should definitely do when we see such AI coding assistant proposals is keep a healthy skepticism in our human programmer minds; there might well be good ideas contained in the code suggestions, but it remains for us humans to decide which those are.

Easy, difficult, and impossible tasks

Some things are difficult or impossible with regular expressions, and many are elegant and highly expressive. The puzzles in this chapter ask you to think about which situation each puzzle describes.

Puzzle 18 *Identifying equal counts*

SUMMARY In this puzzle we would like to balance starting and ending symbols.

At times we encounter a message or a stream that uses balanced "increment" and "decrement" symbols. For example, one way to check that a message has terminated might be to match up the increments and decrements. The same concept would apply to many kinds of messages and symbols—perhaps you would like to set the table with the same number of forks and knives, for example.

As a simplification of the general problem, write a regular expression that matches strings that consist of any number of A characters, followed by the same number of B characters.

For example `AAABBB` and `AAAAAAABBBBBBB` should match, while `AAAABBBBBB` should fail to match.

Author thoughts   *Lateral thinking might help you find the answer*

You cannot match patterns based on having an equal number of different symbols using regular expressions. Or at least you cannot do so in the general case. It is, of course, perfectly possible to require exactly seven A's and exactly seven B's. But if the count is arbitrarily large, the kind of "machine" that can match the message requires additional power.

In computer science or mathematical terms, a regular expression is equivalent to a *nondeterministic finite automaton* (NFA), where a regex provides a very compact spelling of such an NFA. More powerful machines include *pushdown automata* (PDA) which have an indefinitely large "stack" of stored symbols. One most often encounters PDAs as parsers. A PDA, even the nondeterministic variety, remains formally less powerful than a Turing Machine.

In simple terms, if you want to count occurrences, you need to use variables that can store a number (or a data structure like a list to hold the symbols).

Many new users of regexen fall into a trap of hoping this puzzle is solvable. Or more often still, something equivalent like matching up opening and closing parentheses, brackets, or XML/HTML tags. However, regular expressions do not contain variables or data structures, notwithstanding the other kinds of complexity they do encompass.

AI thoughts   *Hic sunt dracones*

Current AI coding assistants fail to notice the dragons here. In fact, both Copilot and ChatGPT go wrong in *exactly* the same way for this puzzle. Of the two, ChatGPT, as usual, acts much more confident about its error.

Copilot gives a compact, straightforward, and wrong answer to the comment I created:

```
# This regular expression only matches strings that consist
# of any number of 'A' characters, followed by the same
# number of 'B' characters.
pattern = re.compile(r'^(A+)(B+)$')
```

This pattern only matches one-or-more A's followed by one-or-more B's. Nothing constrains their number to be the same.

Given the same prompt, ChatGPT replies:

ChatGPT response

Here is a regular expression that will only match strings that consist of any number of A characters followed by the same number of B characters:

```
^(A+)(B+)$
```

This regular expression uses the ^ and $ symbols to anchor the pattern to the start and end of the string, respectively. The A+ and B+ patterns match one or more A or B characters, respectively. The parentheses around each pattern capture the matched characters, so that you can access them later if needed.

Here are some examples of strings that will match this regular expression:

- AB
- AAB
- AAABBB
- AAAABBBB

And here are some examples of strings that will not match:

- A (does not have any B characters)
- B (does not have any A characters)
- AAAB (has more A characters than B characters)
- AABBB (has more B characters than A characters)

What is so intriguing about this error is that in some metaphorical way, the AI "understands" what I asked it, yet produces incorrect code. It is actually true that AAABB will match the regular expression, as claimed, although obviously it is not a pattern that *should* be matched. But the description of the patterns that allegedly do not match is surprisingly true to the requested behavior. Of course, the AIs' (both of them) proposed regular expression actually *will* match AAAB and AABBB. Yet somehow the context that those *should not* match was correctly extracted from the request.

As a very small quibble, logicians will point out that "any number of A characters" should include zero of them. So perhaps * is a more appropriate quantifier than +; but I think even ordinary English is ambiguous about which would be the preferred behavior from the description I provided.

Puzzle 19   **Matching before duplicate words**

> **SUMMARY**   Match initial prefixes that avoid duplication within full
> strings.

If you looked at the last puzzle, you saw that some match patterns you might anticipate to be possible with regular expressions are not expressible with regexen. Think about whether this puzzle is possible and, if so, how. It might not be possible, and the hypothetical `pat` in the examples shown might not exist.

Write a regular expression that will match all the initial words of a string (including any punctuation or spacing that might surround words), stopping before any word that is duplicated in the string. For example:

```
s1 = "this and that not other"
assert re.match(pat, s1).group() == s1
```

Note that `re.match()` always starts at the beginning of a string when looking for a match. If you preferred `re.search()` you would need to begin the pattern with `^`. In the first example no word is duplicated in the phrase, and therefore the entire phrase matches. In contrast:

```
s2 = "this and that and other"
assert re.match(pat, s2).group() == 'this '
```

The second example is a little different. The first word `this` never reoccurs. But the second word `and` does occur later in the phrase, and therefore it, and everything following the duplicated word, must be excluded.

Author thoughts   **Find a pattern that will fulfill the requirement**

This match pattern is indeed possible to write as a regular expression. We need to use backreferences to check it, but those are a standard feature of regular expression engines:

```
((\w+\b)(?!.*\2\b)\W*)+
```

As well as the backreference, we use a negative lookahead assertion. That is, the basic thing being matched is `(\w+\b) \W*) +`. That is to say, match one or more alphanumeric characters `\w` followed by a word boundary. That "word" might be followed by zero or more non-alphanumeric characters. Then overall, match one or more repetitions of that general pattern. If the alphanumeric class seems too broad, you could instead limit it to `[A-Za-z]` without changing the general concept.

So far, so good. But we have not excluded the repeated words. We do that with the negative lookahead, `(?!.*\2\b)`.

That is, we want to look through the entire rest of the string being evaluated, and make sure that we do not encounter the same word currently matched. The initial `.*` just matches any number of characters, but the `\2` is the actual current word. We still use word boundary in the negative lookahead because a longer word of which the current word is a prefix would be permitted.

Keep in mind how groups are numbered. Since there are parentheses surrounding the entire expression (other than the + quantifier), that whole thing is group 1. So the first subpattern inside of that, matching the current word, is group 2, hence named as `\2`.

AI thoughts **Deep fakes in the Chomsky hierarchy**

The prompt I used for ChatGPT on this puzzle is:

Please write a regular expression that will match all the initial words of a string (including any punctuation or spacing that might surround words), stopping before any word that is duplicated in the string.

I have reproduced the entire rather detailed response from the AI, because it contains quite a lot that is intriguingly right and foolishly wrong.

ChatGPT response

Here is a regular expression that will match all the initial words of a string, stopping before any word that is duplicated in the string:

`\b(\w+)\b(?!.*\b\1\b)`

Explanation:

- \b is a word boundary, which matches the position between a word character (as defined by \w) and a non-word character.
- (\w+) is a capture group that matches one or more word characters (letters, digits, or underscores). The capture group is used to capture the matched word.
- (?!...) is a negative lookahead assertion, which means that the regular expression should not match if the pattern inside the lookahead is found immediately following the current position.
- .* is a wildcard that matches any character (except a newline) zero or more times.
- \b is a word boundary, as described above.
- \1 is a backreference to the first capture group, which refers to the word matched by (\w+).
- \b is a word boundary, as described above.

This regular expression will match the first word in the string, followed by any subsequent words that do not appear earlier in the string. If a word appears earlier in the string, the negative lookahead assertion will cause the regular expression to stop matching.

For example, the regular expression will match the following strings:

- "The quick brown fox" (match: "The quick brown")
- "foo bar baz" (match: "foo bar")

But it will not match the following strings:

- "foo bar foo" (no match)
- "The quick brown the" (no match)

Where to begin? The pattern provided is mostly correct. In particular, it captures the main idea of using a negative lookahead assertion. It is not entirely correct because it will only ever match either the first word (if that is never repeated) or nothing at all (if it *is* repeated).

It is straightforward to improve ChatGPT's answer by surrounding the regex with some extra parentheses and quantifying the whole group with either * or +. The only difference is whether we want to return an empty string or a None in the case the first word is repeated; either is a reasonable interpretation of the puzzle statement.

Moreover, the detailed explanation ChatGPT provides of each element of the regular expression is well phrased and correct. I am not sure why this prompt produced such a detailed description of each small element of the regex whereas many other prompts produced much less verbose responses. Perhaps the AI was proud of its cleverness in finding a negative lookahead approach, and felt more loquacious.

What is much more puzzling to me is that in the last puzzle, the regex was wrong but the explanations and examples were mostly correct. Here, however, the regex is (mostly) correct, but the explanation and examples are complete nonsense.

The string "The quick brown fox" should match in its entirety per the stated goal, but would match only "The" in the regular expression suggested. So claiming to match "The quick brown" is wrong on both counts. The "foo bar baz" example is wrong in pretty much the same way.

The AI is actually correct about "foo bar foo" matching either under the stated goal or under the pattern provided. However, it is mildly wrong about "The quick brown the." That said, if we were to adjust the pattern to be case-insensitive, "The" and "the" would be word repetition and hence there would be no match; the AI has come across an inkling of a sensible example with that negative one.

Puzzle 20 *Testing an IPv4 address*

SUMMARY   As a practical use, match the format of IPv4 addresses.

"Internet protocol version 4" addresses are prevalent in almost everything we do with computers. "Under the hood" (so to speak), an IPv4 address is just a 32-bit unsigned integer. However, it is universal to write them in a human-memorable way as "dotted quads." In that format, each byte of the address is represented as a decimal number between 0 and 255 (the range of an integer byte), and the four bytes are separated by periods.

Some particular address ranges have special or reserved meanings, but they remain IPv4 addresses and should be matched for this puzzle. Can you write a regular expression to test if a string is a valid IPv4 address? Some examples:

- Valid: 192.168.20.1
- Invalid: 292.168.10.1
- Invalid: 5.138.0.21.23
- Invalid: 192.AA.20.1

The first of these is a good address; it happens to be a range reserved for internal addresses within an organization (usually one particular router), and hence exists in many local networks. The others fail for various reasons.

The first invalid address contains numbers outside the permitted integer range in one quad. The second invalid address has five dotted elements rather than four. The third invalid address contains characters other than decimal digits in one of the quads.

Author thoughts   **Ask whether regexen are powerful enough for a problem**

It would be very easy to match naive *dotted quads* that simply consisted of four numbers with up to three digits, separated by dots. You might express that as:

```
^(\d{1,3}\.){3}\d{1,3}$
```

This code will indeed match every IPv4 address. But it will also match many things that are invalid, such as `992.0.100.13`. Matching three-digit numbers that begin with 3-9 are definitely wrong. We can try to fix that oversight by allowing only acceptable hundreds digits:

```
^([12]?\d{1,2}\.){3}[12]?\d{1,2}$
```

This has far fewer false positives. It says "maybe start with a 1 or a 2, then follow that by one or two more digits" (repeating that for dotted quads). So far, so good: `992.0.100.13` is ruled out. But we still might accept `271.10.199.3` which has an invalid first quad.

 To fix the pattern we have to bite the bullet and list all and only quads we can allow. That is, if a quad starts with a 25 and has three digits, the next digit can only be 0-5. And if it starts with a 2 it definitely cannot have a digit more than 5 next.

```
^((25[0-5]|2[0-4]\d|[01]?\d\d?)\.){3}(25[0-5]|2[0-4]\d|[01]?\d\d?)$
```

The pattern is a bit of a mouthful, but when we see how it is built up, the pattern becomes quite clear and elegant. All the stuff after the number quantifier `{3}` is just a repetition of the earlier subpattern. This is simply because we match three numbers that are followed by a period, but the final number must not be followed by anything.

The main subpattern is just an alternation of options. Maybe the quad looks like 25[0-5]. Or maybe it looks like 2[0-4]\d. These describe all the valid numbers in the 200+ range. For the rest, we get a little clever.

If the quad is not three digits beginning with a 2, it can either be three-digits beginning with 1 or 0. Conventionally, leading zeros are dropped, but that is not required. However, two-digit or one-digit numbers are also common; any such two- or one-digit numbers are permitted. So we make the initial [01] optional, and also make the final digit optional with \d?. This gives all and only the remaining permissible quads.

AI thoughts   *I want to be a machine*

This problem is one where, at the moment of writing, different AI coding assistants vary in quality. During my first try at using Copilot with the code comment "Match an IPv4 address," I was given the suggestion of:

```
re.compile(r'(?P<first>\d+)\.(?P<second>\d+)\.' +
           r'(?P<third>\d+)\.(?P<fourth>\d+)')
```

This suggestion is fairly terrible. It will indeed match every IPv4 address, but it will also match every dotted-quad-like string with at least one digit per position. For example, 56789.1.0.0987654 would purportedly be an IPv4 address here.

It is also *interesting* that Copilot suggested using named groups for the portions of the IPv4 address. This could very well often be a good idea for later working with, e.g., a /16 or /24 subnet based on the address provided; however, that potential need was not anything I indicated in my prompt.

However, I gave Copilot another try a few days later (and within a GitHub Codespace rather than within my local Neovim plugin; this should not matter, but who knows). In this second try, Copilot came up with a slightly better answer of:

```
re.compile(r"""
    (\d{1,3})\.(\d{1,3})\.(\d{1,3})\.(\d{1,3})
    # Match 4 groups of 1-3 digits""", re.VERBOSE)
```

Notice that the code comment was written by Copilot, not by me. This answer is still *wrong*, but it excludes many false positives that the first answer would accept by only allowing digit sequences of length 1-3.

ChatGPT completed this task remarkably well. My initial prompt to it was "Write a regular expression to match an IPv4 address." This prompt produced the common response of "I'm sorry [...] I am a large language model [...] and my knowledge is limited."

I tried modifying my prompt to:

Write a Python program to match an IPv4 address.

Its response began with "Here is a Python program that uses regular expressions to match an IPv4 address." For a human, the contrast in responses was humorous. But the AI produced a really excellent function, accompanied by both excellent test cases and a very clear English language description of *why* this code was used:

```
def match_ipv4_address(string):
    regex = r"\b(?:(?:25[0-5]|2[0-4][0-9]" \
                r"|1[0-9][0-9]" \
                r"|[1-9]?[0-9])\.){3}" \
            r"(?:25[0-5]|2[0-4][0-9]|1[0-9][0-9]|[1-9]?[0-9])\b"
    return re.search(regex, string) is not None

print(match_ipv4_address("192.168.1.1"))        # True
print(match_ipv4_address("1.1.1.1"))            # True
print(match_ipv4_address("255.255.255.255"))    # True
print(match_ipv4_address("0.0.0.0"))            # True
print(match_ipv4_address("invalid_ip"))         # False
```

I would quibble about a few elements of the produced regular expression at code-review, but the code is *substantially correct*. For example, `'+\d{2}+'` feels both more expressive and more compact to me than `[0-9][0-9]`. In a pedantic mood, I might also note that the Unicode category "Decimal Number (Nd)" includes characters other than only Western Arabic numerals, and arguably an IPv4 address should allow those.

Puzzle 21 **Matching a numeric sequence**

> **SUMMARY**   Match sequences that represent successive numeric doubling.

Here's a giveaway for you. This puzzle is *possible* to solve. I do not give you that same assurance when I describe the next three (related) puzzles.

Regular expressions do not really understand numbers. A 7 or a 777 might be sequences of digits matched in a string, but they are not fundamentally different, to regexen, than any other character patterns. Quantifiers can express numbers, either 0/1 with ?, 0 or more with *, or 1 or more with +. In extended regexen like Python uses, we can even express specific counts like {3,6} for "at least three and not more than 6." But those are specific numbers, not calculated quantities.

Nonetheless, we would like to recognize a distinct integer sequence and rule out other integer sequences, using a regular expression. The trick here is that we can represent an integer as repetitions of the same character, and the number of such repetitions can (to us, at least) represent numbers.

Specifically, for this puzzle, you would like to identify strings that represent successive doublings and exclude all strings that do not have that pattern. We use the symbol @ for one unit simply because it is available and does not have special meaning within regex patterns. Spaces can separate numbers from each other. So for example:

```
>>> s1 = "@@@ @@@@@@ @@@@@@@@@@@@ "              ◄──────── 3 6 12
>>> s2 = "@ @@ @@@@ @@@@@@@@ @@@@@@@@@@@@@@@@ " ◄── 1 2 4 8 16
>>> s3 = "@@ @@@@ @@@@@ @@@@@@@@@@ "             ◄────────── 2 4 5 10
>>> s4 = "@ @ @@ @@@@ "                          ◄──────────── 1 1 2 4
>>> for s in (s1, s2, s3, s4):
...     match = re.search(pat, s)
...     if match
...         print("VALID", match.group())
...     else:
...         print("INVALID", s)

VALID @@@ @@@@@@ @@@@@@@@@@@@                    ◄──────────── 3 6 12
VALID @ @@ @@@@ @@@@@@@@ @@@@@@@@@@@@@@@@         ◄──────────── 1 2 4 8 16
INVALID @@ @@@@ @@@@@ @@@@@@@@@@                  ◄──────────── 2 4 5 10
INVALID @ @ @@ @@@@                               ◄──────────── 1 1 2 4
```

The pattern you come up with should match strings of any length that follow the doubling sequence, and should reject strings of any length that fail to follow it all the way to their end. The final "number" in a string will always be followed by a space, otherwise it will not have been terminated and should not match.

Author thoughts   **Rule out the impossible to be left with the solution**

Let's start with the solution, then explain why it works:

```
^(((@+) )(?=\3\3 ))+(\3\3 )$
```

What we do here is several steps:

1. Make sure we are beginning at the start of the string (`^`). This is where s4 failed; it doubles as a suffix, but we are required to start at the beginning.
2. Match at least one `@` symbol, up to however many occur in a row. After that group of `@` symbols, we have a space that is not part of the group.
3. *Lookahead* to a pattern that has twice as many `@` symbols as the group we last saw. I spelled that as `\3\3`, which feels intuitive, but you could likewise spell it as `\3{2}` to mean the same thing.
4. Finally, after all those repetitions of lookaheads and groups, collect the same pattern as the lookahead just before the end of the string. We want to have the entire sequence in `match.group()`, not to leave off the last "number."

AI thoughts   **Wheat and chessboards**

As with a great many of these puzzles, ChatGPT produces a response that is *largely correct*, or contains a grain of a correct idea within it, but is not an actual solution. In itself, merely showing you what is right and what is wrong might be becoming repetitive.

I think this is an opportunity to mention a slightly lateral thought. I can ask one of the AI coding assistants to complete some code I am working on, for which I only have a general prose description of its purpose. Often it will create something which is sort of correct, and that has relatively easily fixed bugs within it. Of course, I need to carefully review the suggestion as an experienced and competent programmer before I accept any such solution.

A provocative point I would make here is to ask how an AI differs, in this respect, from a junior programmer. Unfortunately, as a wizened veteran of many code shops, when I write "junior programmer" I also often mean people with 20+ years experience, and who perhaps have a title like "Senior Development Lead."

The only real solution I would suggest to this conundrum is that *test driven development* is almost always the correct way to develop code bases. Without test coverage—and tests that are actually run as an integral part of the development process—it is essentially impossible to know that code is correct. AI code assistants can also help write tests; but the key feature of a unit test is that it must be *immediately* obvious to any semi-competent reader of it (which also means we need to review unit tests AIs suggest).

My question to the AI in this puzzle was:

Suppose that sequences of integers are represented by repeated characters, separated by a space. For example, the sequence 1, 3, 5 is represented as @ @@@ @@@@@. Please write a regular expression that detects whether such a sequence represents each number doubling the previous one.

ChatGPT response

Here is a regular expression that can detect whether a given string represents a sequence of integers where each number is double the previous one:

```
^@(?: \@{2})*$
```

Explanation:

- `^` and `$` anchor the regular expression to the start and end of the string, respectively.
- `@` matches the character `@`.
- `(?:...)` is a non-capturing group, which means that it groups together a set of patterns but does not capture the matching text as a separate group.
- `\@{2}` matches the character `@` repeated exactly two times.
- `*` after the non-capturing group indicates that the preceding pattern (in this case, `\@{2}`) can be matched zero or more times.

This regular expression will match a string that starts with an `@` character, followed by zero or more occurrences of a space followed by two `@` characters.

There is something right here. The core idea we need to use is indeed a backreference and a quantifier or repetition to indicate that is occurs twice. However, the pattern proposed by ChatGPT will match @ @@ but little else that we actually want. For example, @ @@ @@ @@ will match, but the valid strings @ @@ @@@@ or @@@ @@@@@@ will not. I leave it as an exercise to readers to compare my solution to that suggested by ChatGPT.

In a nod to fairness toward the AI, my request only asked to judge *whether* a pattern matches, not returns the actual match group. With that weaker constraint, there is probably a way to make a non-capturing group work rather than my more elaborate lookahead-plus-suffix approach. I also failed to prompt indicating the required trailing space as delimiter, but I consider that distinction comparatively trivial.

Puzzle 22   **Matching the Fibonacci sequence**

SUMMARY   Match strings representing a particular well-known numeric sequence: the Fibonacci numbers.

Here we get to something harder than the last puzzle. It is not obvious whether regular expressions are powerful enough to express this sequence. Think about your solution or the reasons it is impossible before you turn the page.

The Fibonacci sequence is a famous recursive relationship, in which each number in the sequence is the sum of the prior two numbers. Hence, the first few Fibonacci numbers are:

```
1 1 2 3 5 8 13 21 34 55 89 144
```

In fact, the Fibonacci sequence. is only one of an infinite number of similar recursive sequences, known generally as Lucas sequences. The Lucas numbers are one such sequence in which the initial elements are 2 and 1 (rather than 1 and 1). We are interested here in matching "Fibonacci-like" sequences, where given two elements, the next one is the sum of those prior two.

As in the last puzzle, we represent numeric sequences by a number of repetitions of the @ symbol followed by spaces. For example:

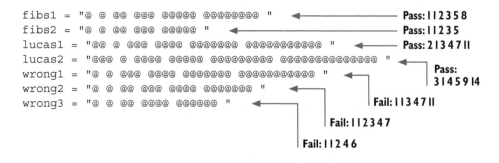

Can you create a regular expression that matches only Fibonacci-like sequences within encoded strings?

Author thoughts   **The Golden Spiral beautifully generalizes Fibonacci numbers**

It turns out that matching properly encoded Fibonacci-like sequences is within the power of regular expressions. Adding together two prior elements is a lot like simply doubling the one prior element as we did in the last puzzle.

The main difference in the solution to this puzzle versus the last one is that we need to backreference two groups in the lookahead pattern rather than just one. Study the explanation of the last puzzle before looking at the solution to this one. This regular expression is complex enough that it demands the verbose form of regular expressions to make sense of it.

Note that in the verbose format, to specify a literal space, we must use \; however, within the lookahead group, we need to use [ ] instead because it gets mistaken for a partial backreference:

```
pat = re.compile(r"""
    ^                    # Start of candidate sequence
    (                    # Group that will be repeated
      ((@+)\ (@+)\ )     # Two blocks of one or more @'s
      (?=$|\3\4[ ])      # Lookahead to concatenation of last two
    )+                   # Repeat numbers plus sum at least once
    (@+\ )?              # Capture the final "number"
    $                    # End of candidate sequence
    """, re.VERBOSE)
```

```
for name, seq in seqs.items():
    match1 = re.search(pat, seq)
    match2 = re.search(pat, seq.split(" ", 1)[1])
    match = match1 and match2
    print("VALID" if match else "INVALID", name, seq)
```

seqs is any dictionary of strings being evaluated (e.g. {"fibs1": fibs1, ...})

Let us look at the output from running that:

```
VALID fibs1 @ @ @@ @@@ @@@@@ @@@@@@@@
VALID fibs2 @ @ @@ @@@ @@@@@
VALID lucas1 @@ @ @@@ @@@@ @@@@@@@ @@@@@@@@@@@
VALID lucas2 @@@ @ @@@@ @@@@@ @@@@@@@@@ @@@@@@@@@@@@@@
INVALID wrong1 @ @ @@@ @@@@ @@@@@@@ @@@@@@@@@@@
INVALID wrong2 @ @ @@ @@@ @@@@ @@@@@@@
INVALID wrong3 @ @ @@ @@@@ @@@@@@
```

This "solution" *did* resort to using a little bit of Python code beyond regular expressions themselves. The problem is that if you only considered the full string, wrong3 would falsely match. Its sequence is 1, 1, 2, 4, 6; and since pat grabs two "numbers" at a time, that only checks that 1+1 equals 2, and that 2+4 equals 6. The fact that 1+2 does not equal 4 is not checked in the single match. By checking both the full sequence, and the tail of the sequence (without the first number) we check everything.

While the very Python-oriented seq.split(" ", 1)[1] is a slight cheat, we could also be more regular expression oriented by creating two patterns, the second of which grabs any initial number, but only quantifies and does lookahead on the tail. Details of that approach are left to the reader.

AI thoughts   *The fractal geometry of nature*

I figured to give the AI coding assistant any chance at all, I should simplify to only ask about Fibonacci rather than the entire Lucas sequence generalization. I asked ChatGPT:

> Using the same encoding of numbers in which N repeated @ symbols represent the number N, please write a regular expression that will detect whether a sequence is the start of the Fibonacci sequence."

Generally, ChatGPT comes up with *some* answer to questions, even where it is completely nonsensical. For example, although completely outside the scope of this book, I have asked ChatGPT to write a Wikipedia article and resume about me (i.e., "David Mertz, Python programmer, etc."). I am not original in this game; I've seen other people do the same before me. The result is something that looks *extremely* verisimilitudinous and relatively well written. In other words, it is what Stephen Colbert jokingly coined as "truthiness" ("seeming true" without being concerned with actual accuracy). Moreover, *several* of the facts ChatGPT invents to describe me happen to be true (because my name really does occur in its training corpora, and nearby to some various phrases likely to appear in resumes and the like). But other purported facts are nonsense factually, and yet very much the *kinds* of things that would appear in a resume. For example, I *did* go to college and grad school; just not at the places invented by ChatGPT (but it chose real schools that I plausibly *could* have gone to).

Let us look at its answer to this prompt:

ChatGPT response

Here is a regular expression that can detect whether a given string represents the start of the Fibonacci sequence:

```
^@(?: @(?!.*@.*@) | @{3,}(?!.*@.*@))*$
```

Explanation:

- `^` and `$` anchor the regular expression to the start and end of the string, respectively.
- `@` matches the character `@`.
- `(?:...)` is a non-capturing group, which means that it groups together a set of patterns but does not capture the matching text as a separate group.
- `@(?!.@.@)` is a positive lookahead assertion. It matches a single `@` character only if it is not followed by two `@` characters anywhere in the string.
- `@{3,}(?!.@.@)` matches three or more `@` characters only if they are not followed by two `@` characters anywhere in the string.
- `*` after the non-capturing group indicates that the preceding pattern (in this case, `@(?!.*@.*@)|@{3,}(?!.*@.*@))` can be matched zero or more times.

This regular expression will match a string that starts with an `@` character, followed by zero or more occurrences of either a single `@` character that is not followed by two `@` characters anywhere in the string, or three or more `@` characters that are not followed by two `@` characters anywhere in the string. This will match strings that represent the start of the Fibonacci sequence.

The "explanation" is partially correct piecewise. Not entirely, for example in describing @ (?!.@.@) as a positive lookahead assertion. It is actually a simple character match followed by a negative lookahead assertion. A lot of the rest of the piecewise explanations hold up though.

However, taken together, it is difficult to make any sense whatsoever of the overall regular expression. Pretty much it is gibberish, but the kind of gibberish that "seem plausible" for a complex regular expression. It is quite possible that the regex simply has reached the point of mental overload for your author, but I cannot think of anything it will match other than @ @ @ (or any number of additional single @ characters after spaces.

To me, this effort by the AI to "just answer, even if it is gibberish" is very similar to the "plausible but nonsense" resume situation I mentioned. I very much encourage readers to email me if they can think of any other pattern the ChatGPT regex might match that I have overlooked. In any case, it certainly will not include anything Fibonacci-like.

Puzzle 23   **Matching the prime numbers**

> **SUMMARY**   Match strings representing the initial finite prefix of the sequence of prime numbers.

Perhaps surprisingly, in the last puzzle we were able to match Fibonacci-like sequences using regular expressions. Let's turn next to whether we might do the same thing with prime numbers. In particular, if you can find it, your regular expression(s) will only need to match ascending initial sequences of the primes, but all such initial sequences.

As in the last two puzzles, we encode numeric sequences using a number of contiguous @ symbols, with each "number" separated by spaces. For example:

```
primes4 = "@@ @@@ @@@@@ @@@@@@@ "                    ◄─────── Match: 2 3 5 7
primes5 = "@@ @@@ @@@@@ @@@@@@@ @@@@@@@@@@@ "  ◄─── Match: 2 3 5 7 11
fail1 = "@@ @@@ @@@@@@@ @@@@@@@@@@@ "              ◄─────── Fail: 2 3 7 11
fail2 = "@@ @@@ @@@@ @@@@@ @@@@@@@ "                ◄─────── Fail: 2 3 4 5 7
```

The Sieve of Eratosthenes is a lovely and ancient algorithm for finding all the prime numbers. It "strikes out" each multiple of a prime as it steps through all the natural numbers, leaving only primes thereby. In a compact Python implementation it can look like the below (this can be made much more efficient, but at the price of more code):

```
def get_primes():
    "Simple lazy Sieve of Eratosthenes"
    candidate = 2
    found = []
    while True:
        if all(candidate % prime != 0 for prime in found):
            yield candidate
            found.append(candidate)
        candidate += 1
```

The form of the Sieve is definitely reminiscent of lookahead assertions which we have used in many of the puzzles. Think about whether you can implement this using regular expressions (do not think about performance for this puzzle). Before you look at the discussion, try either to find a regular expression to match the valid sequences or to formulate clearly why you cannot.

Author thoughts   ***Honor the fundamental theorem of arithmetic***

This puzzle turns out to be another one that exceeds the ability of regular expressions. On the face of it, it might seem like *negative lookahead assertions* are exactly what you would use to implement the Sieve, or something akin to it. That is, if some group matched, e.g., (@@@) or (@+), then you should be able to backreference to a repetition of that group.

Let's say the hypothetical group was number 7. In that case, a negative lookahead assertion like (?! \7{2,}) would state precisely that no contiguous numbers of @"symbols, whose count is a multiple of the number in the prior match group, occur later in the string. That sounds a lot like what the Sieve does.

Negative lookahead is indeed a powerful and useful technique. In fact, you could perfectly well implement a partial sieve to exclude all the multiples of the first N primes from occurring in a candidate string. The problem is that regular expressions can only have a finite number of match groups by definition. That is, regular expressions are a way of expressing *finite state* machines. The exact maximum number of groups can vary between regex engines; it is 100 in the Python standard library re module, 500 in the third-party regex module, and various other numbers in other programming languages or libraries. But it is always a finite number.

To match *every* string of initial primes, we need to "strike out" indefinitely many primes along the way. This same problem would occur for every other sequential prime-finding algorithm. There do exist direct primality tests that do not iterate through the smaller primes, such as the probabilistic Miller-Rabin test[4] or the deterministic Agrawal-Kayal-Saxena test. However, all of those require mathematical calculations that are not possible in regular expressions.

AI thoughts   **Sense and nonsense**

Obviously, given that the problem is impossible to solve, AI coding assistants will not solve it. But gosh, they sure do sound confident in their non-solutions:

> Using the same encoding of numbers in which N repeated @ symbols represent the number N, please write a regular expression that will detect whether a sequence contains all and only a list of initial primes. For example, 2 3 5 7 11 13 should match, but 2 3 13 15 should not.

ChatGPT response

Here is a regular expression that can detect whether a given string represents a list of initial prime numbers:

```
^@(?: @(?!@) | @{3,})(?: @(?!@| @{3,}))*$
```

Explanation:

- ^ and $ anchor the regular expression to the start and end of the string, respectively.
- @ matches the character @.
- (?:...) is a non-capturing group, which means that it groups together a set of patterns but does not capture the matching text as a separate group.
- @(?!@) is a positive lookahead assertion. It matches a single @ character only if it is not followed by another @ character.
- @{3,} matches three or more @ characters.
- (* ?: @(?!@| @{3,}))* is a non-capturing group that matches zero or more occurrences of a space followed by a single @ character that is not followed by another @ character or three or more @ characters.

---

[4]   A version of the Miller-Rabin test can be made deterministic if the Generalized Riemann hypothesis holds.

This regular expression will match a string that starts with an @ character, followed by zero or more occurrences of a space followed by a single @ character that is not followed by another @ character or three or more @ characters. This will match strings that contain a list of initial prime numbers.

As with the last exercise, once ChatGPT goes off into gibberish, it confuses things like positive lookahead with negative lookahead in its "explanation." For the most part, the piecewise explanation is true though; indicating that among the corpora that were used in training were tutorials or explanations of the various primitives of regular expressions.

It is difficult to determine what triggers this particular regular expression, and equally difficult to figure out whether it can match *anything* other than @ @ @ (or more or fewer single @ characters separated by spaces). One might certainly wish that these AI coding assistants had some sort of filter where they simply refused to answer some questions. ChatGPT does this in some cases with its generic "I'm sorry [. . .] I am a large language model [. . .]" and in other cases with sensible content filters like "Such a story would be disturbing and inappropriate to create. Is there something else I can help you with?"

While detecting that a use of ChatGPT as an AI coding assistant had strayed into the realm of pure gibberish might be difficult, it does not feel impossible to engineer such a capability. In general, if the model has very low confidence in its prediction of the next word (or at least in the next reasonably long sequence of words), falling back to a generic "I'm sorry" message would be more useful than producing pure nonsense. Without directly knowing proprietary architecture details, I would guess that performing some kind of threshold filter prior to a softmax layer should be possible within a general transformer architecture.

Puzzle 24 *Matching relative prime numbers*

> **SUMMARY**   Match strings representing sequences of relative prime numbers.

If you read the last puzzle, you saw the subtle reason why a regular expression cannot match an initial sequence of primes. Think *finite* automaton. If you skipped that puzzle, at least go back and refresh your understanding of the Sieve of Eratosthenes.

Mathematics has a concept of *relative primes* which is slightly weaker than primality. All prime numbers are relatively prime—also called *coprime*—with each other, but other pairs are as well. Two coprime numbers have no common divisors other than 1. This is certainly true of prime numbers; for example, 11 and 53 are relatively prime since neither have any divisors other than themselves and 1. But likewise 10 and 21 are coprime since the divisors of the first are 2 and 5, but those of the second are 3 and 7, which do not overlap.

So the question for this puzzle is whether you can create an expression that will identify all and only sequences of ascending natural numbers where all of them are relatively prime to each other. Trivially, any sequence of ascending primes qualifies here, but so do other sequences.

As in the last three puzzles, we encode numeric sequences using a number of contiguous @ symbols, with each "number" separated by spaces. For example:

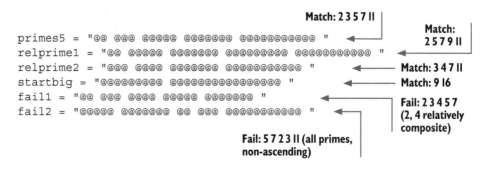

Match: 2 3 5 7 11

Match: 2 5 7 9 11

```
primes5   = "@@ @@@ @@@@@ @@@@@@@ @@@@@@@@@@@ "
relprime1 = "@@ @@@@@ @@@@@@@ @@@@@@@@@ @@@@@@@@@@@ "
relprime2 = "@@@ @@@@ @@@@@@@ @@@@@@@@@@@ "
startbig  = "@@@@@@@@@ @@@@@@@@@@@@@@@@ "
fail1     = "@@ @@@ @@@@ @@@@@ @@@@@@@ "
fail2     = "@@@@@ @@@@@@@ @@ @@@ @@@@@@@@@@ "
```

Match: 3 4 7 11

Match: 9 16

Fail: 2 3 4 5 7 (2, 4 relatively composite)

Fail: 5 7 2 3 11 (all primes, non-ascending)

Are relative primes consigned to the same fate as primes?

Author thoughts   **Nothing is either true or false but thinking makes it so**

There are a couple of issues to consider in this solution. It turns out that such a solution is indeed possible, using much the same style as the Sieve of Eratosthenes, but not an identical technique. That is, as discussed in the last puzzle, we are perfectly well able to reject a string based on a future multiple of a given number.

The trick is that we do not need to reject *infinitely* many if we do not assume that a string needs to contain all the initial primes. Instead, we can focus just on a single number at a time, and rule out *its* multiples. We might miss some primes in our sequence or indeed have some relatively prime composite numbers. But that satisfies the current puzzle.

However, for this "striking through" to work, we need also to enforce the rule that sequences are ascending. Otherwise, we might encounter, e.g., @@@@@@@@ @@@@ @@ (i.e., 8 4 2). Those are definitely not mutually coprime. However, "striking out" multiples of 8 does not help reject 4 later in the string. Python only allows fixed length lookbehind assertions, but some other regex implementation could technically relax this ascending sequence restriction (however, a library that did so would quickly face catastrophic exponential complexity in this case):

```
^((@@+) (?=\2@)(?!.* \2{2,} ))+
```

Here we first identify a group of two or more @ symbols. Then we do a positive lookahead to ensure that the next group of @ symbols has at least one more symbol.

The real crux of this is the *negative lookahead* assertion that we never later see a (space delimited) sequence of two or more copies of the group. This pattern does not capture the final "number" in the sequence; it is just used to provide a true or false answer to whether the sequence matches.

AI thoughts   *Six impossible things before breakfast*

Given the last two puzzles, there is little point in presenting yet another example of an AI going off into gibberish. I can note that in "gibberish mode," ChatGPT "has an inordinate fondness for non-capturing groups and negative lookaheads" when it cannot arrive at meaningful regular expressions.

The particular wrong suggestion ChatGPT arrived at was:

```
^(?:@(?!@)(?: @(?!@))*)*$
```

I have difficulty assigning much meaning to the particular ways in which it is wrong, however. I suppose the most we are likely to get out of these last few outlandish failures is an inspiration to quote a great advocate of the AI revolution:

> *If you can't dazzle them with brilliance, baffle them with bull••••.*

> —*W. C. Fields (or so often misattributed).*

Conclusions

Because AI coding assistants often *feel* so human in their responses and completions, it is enormously tempting to anthropomorphize them and imagine that they have a "mental model" of the computer programs and regexen that they are writing (whether correctly or erroneously).

This belief is, of course, completely wrong. It is not merely wrong in the sense that large language models are built from silicon and linear algebra rather than from ganglia and axons, however. The LLMs of today's AI coding assistants are very specifically *not* "knowledge engines" (also called "expert systems" in some contexts). There *does* exist a different kind of computer system that tries to represent taxonomies, ontologies, inference rules, and other elements that are more closely analogous to "thinking about the problem." These kinds of models are largely creatures of the 2000s, not of the 2020s, but they could come back to prominence. As of the end of 2022, AI coding assistants are simply not those other kinds of models though.

LLMs cannot understand computer programs as *algorithms*, they can merely recognize that large corpora of codebases tend to have particular words and symbols within the general proximity of other words and symbols, and that other combinations are more-or-less prohibited to occur in such syntagmatic relationships. It is, of course, surprising—even shocking—the degree to which merely modeling the syntagma of the things that humans write can so seemingly authentically emulate humans, with no actual underlying representation of pragmatics, semantics, nor even of actual syntax.

We may feel existential dread about how shallow most of what our brains do is. But at the same time, the examples in this book argue rather convincingly, perhaps even *prove,* that humans, at least sometimes, perform wholly different kinds of reasoning that are conceptual rather than entirely structural. I cannot say whether the examples in this book will liberate you or enshakle you, but they are the reality of LLMs at the start of the 2020s.

Of course, this book was written at a snapshot in time. AI coding assistants, as of right now, are *just* LLMs (and basically all are large transformer neural networks). But next year—or next month—other clever scientists and developers may figure out ways to meld LLMs with actual knowledge models, and it is difficult to predict how much more those future technologies will be capable of.

One lesson that I hope readers take away is that often when AI coding assistants give bad answers, the prompts used to get code out of them were themselves ambiguous. In speaking to humans, a huge number of details are merely *assumed* or *enthymematic* rather than explicitly stated. Large language models have some ability to identify these assumptions, but it is limited. This fact is not entirely bad if it winds up forcing human programmers to become more explicit in code documentation in order to get better results from AI coding assistants. This better documentation will inevitably also later be read by other humans who will benefit thereby.

Learning to use regular expressions

A regular expression is a compact way of describing complex patterns in texts. You can use them to search for patterns and, once found, modify the patterns in complex ways. They can also be used to launch programmatic actions that depend on patterns.

Regular expressions are amazingly powerful and deeply expressive. That is the very reason writing them is just as error-prone as writing any other complex programming code. It is always better to solve a genuinely simple problem simply; when you go beyond simple, think about regular expressions.

For purposes of presenting examples in this tutorial, regular expressions will be surrounded by forward slashes. This style of delimiting regular expressions is used by `sed`, `awk`, Perl, JavaScript, and other tools. For instance, an example might show:

```
/[A-Z]+(abc|xyz)*/
```

The actual regular expression is everything between the slashes. Many examples will be accompanied by an illustration that shows a regular expression, and a text that is highlighted for every match on that expression.

The concise style of these tools focuses on *just* the regular expression better than surrounding it with Python code, such as:

```
import re
pat = re.compile(r"[A-Z]+(abc_xyz)*")
results = re.match(pat, s)
```

What tools use regular expressions?

A large number of tools incorporate regular expressions as part of their functionality. UNIX-oriented command line tools like `grep`, `sed`, and `awk` are mostly wrappers for regular expression processing. Many text editors allow search and/or replacement based on regular expressions. Many programming languages, especially scripting languages such as Ruby, JavaScript, Perl, Python, and TCL, build regular expressions into the heart of the language. Even most command-line shells, such as `bash`, `zsh`, or Windows Powershell allow restricted regular expressions as part of their command syntax.

There are a few variations in regular expression syntax between different tools that use them. Some tools add enhanced capabilities that are not available everywhere. In general, for the simplest cases, this tutorial will use examples based around `grep` or `sed`. For a few more exotic capabilities, Perl or Python examples will be chosen. For the most part, examples will work anywhere, but check the documentation on your own tool for syntax variations and capabilities.

Matching patterns in text: The basics

We begin by explaining and demonstrating literals, escapes, special characters, wildcards, grouping, backreferences, character classes, the complement operator, alternation, and simple quantification.

That probably seems like a mouthful, and indeed you can do quite powerful operations with nothing other than "the basics."

Character literals

```
/a/
```

Mary had **a** little lamb.

And everywhere th**a**t Mary

went, the l**a**mb w**a**s sure

to go.

```
/Mary/
```

Mary had a little lamb.

And everywhere that **Mary**

went, the lamb was sure

to go.

The very simplest pattern matched by a regular expression is a literal character or a sequence of literal characters. Anything in the target text that consists of exactly those characters in exactly the order listed will match. A lowercase character is not identical to its uppercase version, and vice versa. A space in a regular expression, by the way, matches a literal space in the target (this is unlike most programming languages or command-line tools, where spaces separate keywords).

Escaped characters literals

```
/.*/
```

Special characters like .* must be escaped.

```
/\.\*/
```

Special characters like **.*** must be escaped.

In the second example, only the `.*` is highlighted. Several characters have special meanings to regular expressions. A symbol with a special meaning can be matched, but to do so you must prefix it with the backslash character (this includes the backslash character itself: to match one backslash in the target, your regular expression should include `\\`).

Positional special characters

`/^Mary/`

Mary had a little lamb.

And everywhere that Mary

went, the lamb was sure

to go.

`/Mary$/`

Mary had a little lamb.

And everywhere that **Mary**

went, the lamb was sure

to go.

Two special characters are used in almost all regular expression tools to mark the beginning and end of a line: caret (`^`) and dollarsign (`$`). To match a caret or dollar sign as a literal character, you must escape it (i.e., precede it by a backslash).

An interesting thing about the caret and dollarsign is that they match zero-width patterns. That is the length of the string matched by a caret or dollarsign by itself is zero (but the rest of the regular expression can still depend on the zero-width match). Many regular expression tools provide another zero-width pattern for word-boundary (`\b`). Words might be divided by whitespace like spaces, tabs, newlines, or other characters like nulls; the word-boundary pattern matches the actual point where a word starts or ends, not the particular whitespace characters.

The "wildcard" character

`/.a/`

> **Ma**ry **had** a little **la**mb.
>
> And everywhere **that Mar**y
>
> went, the **la**mb **wa**s sure
>
> to go.

In regular expressions, a period can stand for any character. Normally, the newline character is not included, but most tools have optional switches to force inclusion of the newline character also. Using a period in a pattern is a way of requiring that "something" occurs here, without having to decide what.

Users who are familiar with command-line "glob" wildcards will know the question mark as filling the role of "some character" in command masks. But in regular expressions, the question mark has a different meaning, and the period is used as a wildcard.

Grouping regular expressions

`/(Mary)( )(had)/`

> **Mary had** a little lamb.
>
> And everywhere that Mary
>
> went, the lamb was sure
>
> to go.

A regular expression can have literal characters in it, and also zero-width positional patterns. Each literal character or positional pattern is an atom in a regular expression. You may also group several atoms together into a small regular expression that is part of a larger regular expression. One might be inclined to call such a grouping a "molecule," but normally it is also called an atom.

In older UNIX-oriented tools like `grep`, subexpressions must be grouped with escaped parentheses, e.g., `/\(Mary\)/`. In Perl, Python, Ruby, JavaScript, Julia, Rust, Go, and most recent tools (including `egrep`), grouping is done with bare parentheses, but matching a literal parenthesis requires escaping it in the pattern (the example to the side follows Perl).

Using groups for backreferences

The prior example showed match groups, but in themselves they do not affect the text that is matched. Where groups become relevant is when they are used as *a backreference* for substitutions:

```
s/(Mary)( )(had)/\1\2ate/
```

Mary **ate** a little lamb.

And everywhere that Mary

went, the lamb was sure

to go.

Groups 1 and 2 (`Mary` and a space) are referenced in the substitution, but group 3 is not, while the replacement instead adds the string `ate`.

Character classes

```
/[a-z]a/
```

Mary **ha**d a little **la**mb.

And everywhere **tha**t Mary

went, the **la**mb **wa**s sure

to go.

Rather than name only a single character, you can include a pattern in a regular expression that matches any of a set of characters.

A set of characters can be given as a simple list inside square brackets, e.g., `/[aeiou]/` will match any single lowercase vowel. For letter or number ranges you may also use only the first and last letter of a range, with a dash in the middle, e.g., / [A-Ma-m] / will match any lowercase or uppercase in the first half of the alphabet.

Many regular expression tools also provide escape-style shortcuts to the most commonly used character class, such as \s for a whitespace character and \d for a digit. You could always define these character classes with square brackets, but the shortcuts can make regular expressions more compact and more readable.

Complement operator

/ [^a-z] a/

> **Ma**ry had **a** little lamb.
>
> And everywhere that **Ma**ry
>
> went, the lamb was sure
>
> to go.

The caret symbol can actually have two different meanings in regular expressions. Most of the time, it means matching the zero-length pattern for line beginnings. But if it is used at the beginning of a character class, it reverses the meaning of the character class. Everything not included in the listed character set is matched.

For comparison, we can use the beginning-of-line meaning combined with the complement meaning:

/^ [^a-z] [a-z] /

> **Ma**ry had a little lamb.
>
> **An**d everywhere that Mary
>
> went, the lamb was sure
>
> to go.

Here the lines that begin with something other than a lowercase ASCII letter (uppercase letters here), and the one subsequent lowercase letter are matched.

Alternation of patterns

```
/cat|dog|bird/
```

> The pet store sold **cat**s, **dog**s, and **bird**s.

In the next few examples, the character # is just a plain character with no special meaning to regular expressions. Some other punctuation or letter character could be substituted to illustrate the same concepts.

```
/=first|second=/
```

> **=first** first= # =second **second=** # **=first=** # =**second=**

```
/(=)(first)|(second)(=)/
```

> **=first** first= # =second **second=** # **=first=** # =**second=**

```
/=(first|second)=/
```

> =first first= # =second second= # **=first=** # **=second=**

Using character classes is a way of indicating that either one thing or another thing can occur in a particular spot. But what if you want to specify that either of two whole subexpressions occurs in a position in the regular expression? For that, you use the alternation operator, the vertical bar "|". This is the symbol that is also used to indicate a pipe in most command-line shells, and is sometimes called the pipe character.

The pipe character in a regular expression indicates an alternation between everything in the group enclosing it. What this means is that even if there are several groups to the left and right of a pipe character, the alternation greedily asks for everything on both sides. To select the scope of the alternation, you must define a group that encompasses the patterns that may match. These examples illustrate such.

The basic abstract quantifier

`/X(a#a)*X/`

> Match with zero in the middle: **XX** Subexpresion occurs, but: Xa#aABCX Lots of
> occurrences: **Xa#aa#aa#aa#aX** Must repeat entire pattern: Xa#aa#a#aa#aX

One of the most powerful and common things you can do with regular
expressions is to specify how many times an atom occurs in a complete regular expression. Sometimes you want to specify something about the occurrence of a single character, but very often you are interested in specifying
the occurrence of a character class or a grouped subexpression.

There is only one quantifier included with "basic" regular expression syntax, the asterisk *; in English this has the meaning "some or none" or "zero
or more." If you want to specify that any number of an atom may occur as
part of a pattern, follow the atom by an asterisk.

Without quantifiers, grouping expressions does not really serve as much
purpose, but once we can add a quantifier to a subexpression we can say
something about the occurrence of the subexpression as a whole.

Matching patterns in text: Intermediate

For intermediate topics, we move on to additional quantifiers, including
numeric quantifiers, backreferences, and generally good habits and special
tricks for accurately refining your regular expressions.

More abstract quantifiers

`/A+B*C?D/`

AAAD

ABBBBCD

BBBCD

ABCCD

AAABBBC

In a certain way, the lack of any quantifier symbol after an atom quantifies the atom anyway: it says the atom occurs exactly once. Extended regular expressions (which most tools support) add a few other useful numbers to "once exactly" and "zero or more times." The plus sign + means "one or more times" and the question mark ? means "zero or one times." These quantifiers are by far the most common enumerations you will wind up naming.

If you think about it, you can see that the extended regular expressions do not actually let you "say" anything the basic ones do not. They just let you say it in a shorter and more readable way. For example, `(ABC)+` is equivalent to `(ABC)(ABC)*`; and `X(ABC)?Y` is equivalent to `XABCY|XY`. If the atoms being quantified are themselves complicated grouped subexpressions, the question mark and plus-sign can make things *a lot* shorter.

Numeric quantifiers

`/a{5} b{,6} c{4,8}/`

aaaaa bbbbb ccccc

aaa bbb ccc

aaaaa bbbbbbbbbbbbbb ccccc

`/a+ b{3,} c?/`

aaaaa bbbbb ccccc

aaa bbb ccc

aaaaa bbbbbbbbbbbbbb ccccc

`/a{5} b{6,} c{4,8}/`

aaaaa bbbbb ccccc

aaa bbb ccc

aaaaa bbbbbbbbbbbbbb ccccc

Using extended regular expressions, you can specify arbitrary pattern occurrence counts using a more verbose syntax than the question mark, plus sign, and asterisk quantifiers. The curly braces, { and }, can surround a precise count of how many occurrences you are looking for.

The most general form of the curly brace quantification uses two range arguments (the first must be no larger than the second, and both must be non-negative integers). The occurrence count is specified this way to fall between the minimum and maximum indicated (inclusive). As shorthand, either argument may be left empty: if so the minimum/maximum is specified as zero/infinity, respectively. If only one argument is used (with no comma in there), exactly that number of occurrences are matched.

Backreferences

```
/(abc|xyz) \1/
```

jkl abc xyz

jkl xyz abc

jkl **abc abc**

jkl **xyz xyz**

```
/(abc|xyz) (abc|xyz)/
```

jkl **abc xyz**

jkl **xyz abc**

jkl **abc abc**

jkl **xyz xyz**

One powerful option in creating search patterns is specifying that a subexpression that was matched earlier in a regular expression is matched again later in the expression. We do this using backreferences. Backreferences are named by the numbers 1 through 9, preceded by the backslash/escape character when used in this manner. These backreferences refer to each successive group in the match pattern, as in /(one)(two)(three)/\1\2\3/.

Each numbered backreference refers to the group that, in this example, has the word corresponding to the number.

It is important to note something the example illustrates. What gets matched by a backreference is the same literal string matched the first time, even if the pattern that matched the string could have matched other strings. Simply repeating the same grouped subexpression later in the regular expression does not match the same targets as using a backreference.

Backreferences refer back to whatever occurred in the previous grouped expressions, in the order those grouped expressions occurred. Because of the naming convention (\1-\9), many tools limit you to nine backreferences. Some tools allow actual naming of backreferences and/or saving them to program variables. The more advanced parts of this tutorial touch on these topics.

Do not match more than you want to

`/th.*s/`

I want to match **the words that s**tart

with **'th' and end with 's'**.

this

thus

thistle

this line matches too much

Quantifiers in regular expressions are greedy. That is, they match as much as they possibly can.

Probably the easiest mistake to make in composing regular expressions is to match too much. When you use a quantifier, you want it to match everything (of the right sort) up to the point where you want to finish your match. But when using the *, +, or numeric quantifiers, it is easy to forget that the last bit you are looking for might occur later in a line than the one you are interested in.

Tricks for restraining matches

`/th[^s]*./`

> I want to match **the words that s**tart
>
> wi**th 'th' and end with 's'**.
>
> **this**
>
> **thus**
>
> **this**tle
>
> **this** line matches too much

Often if you find that your regular expressions are matching too much, a useful procedure is to reformulate the problem in your mind. Rather than thinking about "what am I trying to match later in the expression?" ask yourself "what do I need to avoid matching in the next part?" Often this leads to more parsimonious pattern matches. Often the way to avoid a pattern is to use the complement operator and a character class. Look at the example, and think about how it works.

The trick here is that there are two different ways of formulating almost the same sequence. You can either think you want to keep matching until you get to XYZ, or you can think you want to keep matching unless you get to XYZ. These are subtly different.

For people who have thought about basic probability, the same pattern occurs. The chance of rolling a 6 on a die in one roll is $1/6$. What is the chance of rolling a 6 in six rolls? A naive calculation puts the odds at $1/6 + 1/6 + 1/6 + 1/6 + 1/6 + 1/6$, or 100%. This is wrong, of course (after all, the chance after twelve rolls is not 200%). The correct calculation is "how do I avoid rolling a 6 for six rolls?"—i.e., $5/6 \times 5/6 \times 5/6 \times 5/6 \times 5/6 \times 5/6$, or about 33%. The chance of getting a 6 is the same chance as not avoiding it (or about 66%). In fact, if you imagine transcribing a series of dice rolls, you could apply a regular expression to the written record, and similar thinking applies.

Tricks for restraining matches better

```
/\bth[a-z]*s\b/
```

> I want to match the words that start
>
> with 'th' and end with 's'.
>
> **this**
>
> **thus**
>
> thistle
>
> **this** line matches too much

Notwithstanding the last section suggesting using negative character classes, it still did not match the goal described of matching *words* starting with "th" and ending with "s". It only did very slightly better than the completely naive approach. Using the zero-width word boundary match is a good approach to accomplish that.

Comments on modification tools

Not all tools that use regular expressions allow you to modify target strings. Some simply locate the matched pattern; the most widely used regular expression tool is probably grep, which is a tool for searching only. Text editors, for example, may or may not allow replacement in their regular expression search facility. As always, consult the documentation on your individual tool.

Of the tools that allow you to modify target text, there are a few differences to keep in mind. The way you specify replacements will vary between tools: a text editor might have a dialog box; command-line tools will use delimiters between match and replacement and programming languages will typically call functions with arguments for match and replacement patterns.

Another important difference to keep in mind is what is getting modified. UNIX-oriented command-line tools typically utilize pipes and STDOUT for changes to buffers, rather than modify files in-place. Using a sed command, for example, will write the modifications to the console, but will not change the original target file (GNU sed adds an --in-place switch). Text editors or programming languages are more likely to modify a file in-place.

A note on modification examples

For purposes of this tutorial, examples will continue to use the `sed` style slash delimiters. Specifically, the examples will indicate the substitution command and the global modifier, as with `s/this/that/g`. This expression means: Replace the string `this` with the string `that` everywhere in the target text.

Examples will consist of the modification command, an input line, and an output line. The output line will have any changes emphasized. Also, each input/output line will be preceded by a less-than or greater-than symbol to help distinguish them (the order will be as described also), which is suggestive of redirection symbols in Unix shells, and some `diff` output styles.

A literal-string modification example

`s/cat/dog/g`

> < The zoo had wild dogs, bobcats, lions, and other wild cats.
>
> > The zoo had wild dogs, bob**dogs**, lions, and other wild **dogs**.

Let us take a look at a couple of modification examples that build on what we have already covered. This one simply substitutes some literal text for some other literal text. The search-and-replace capability of many tools can do this much, even without using regular expressions.

A pattern-match modification example

`s/cat|dog/snake/g`

> < The zoo had wild dogs, bobcats, lions, and other wild cats.
>
> > The zoo had wild **snakes**, bob**snakes**, lions, and other wild **snakes**.

`s/[a-z]+i[a-z]*/nice/g`

> < The zoo had wild dogs, bobcats, lions, and other wild cats.

> The zoo had **nice** dogs, bobcats, **nice**, and other **nice** cats.

Most of the time, if you are using regular expressions to modify a target text, you will want to match more general patterns than just literal strings. Whatever is matched is what gets replaced (even if it is several different strings in the target).

Modification using backreferences

```
s/([A-Z])([0-9]{2,4}) /\2:\1 /g
```

< A37 B4 C107 D54112 E1103 XXX

> **37:A** B4 **107:C** D54112 **1103:E** XXX

It is nice to be able to insert a fixed string everywhere a pattern occurs in a target text. But frankly, doing that is not very context-sensitive. A lot of times, we do not want just to insert fixed strings, but rather to insert something that bears much more relation to the matched patterns. Fortunately, backreferences come to our rescue here. You can use backreferences in the pattern-matches themselves, but it is even more useful to be able to use them in replacement patterns. By using replacement backreferences, you can pick and choose from the matched patterns to use just the parts you are interested in.

To aid readability, subexpressions are grouped with bare parentheses (as with Perl), rather than with escaped parentheses (as with sed).

Another warning on mismatching

This tutorial has already warned about the danger of matching too much with your regular expression patterns. But the danger is so much more serious when you do modifications that it is worth repeating. If you replace a pattern that matches a larger string than you thought of when you composed the pattern, you have potentially deleted some important data from your target.

It is always a good idea to try out your regular expressions on diverse target data that is representative of your production usage. Make sure you are matching what you think you are matching. A stray quantifier or wildcard can make a surprisingly wide variety of texts match what you thought was a specific pattern. And sometimes you just have to stare at your pattern for a while or find another set of eyes to figure out what is really going on even after you see what matches. Familiarity might breed contempt, but it also instills competence.

Advanced regular expression extensions

Buried inside the dense language of regular expressions are many very sophisticated ways of expressing what you wish to match. These include non-greedy quantifiers, atomic groups and possessive quantifiers, lookahead lookbehind assertions, and in many dialects named backreferences and a verbose (and somewhat more readable) format for regular expressions.

About advanced features

Some very useful enhancements are included in some regular expression tools. These enhancements often make the composition and maintenance of regular expression considerably easier. But check with your own tool to see what is supported.

The programming language Perl is probably the most sophisticated tool for regular expression processing, which explains much of its erstwhile popularity. The examples illustrated will use Perl-ish code to explain concepts. Other programming languages, especially other scripting languages such as Python, have a similar range of enhancements. But for purposes of illustration, Perl's syntax most closely mirrors the regular expression tools it builds on, such as `ed`, `ex`, `grep`, `sed`, and `awk`.

Non-greedy quantifiers

`/th.*s/`

I want to match **the words that s**tart

wi**th 'th' and end with 's'**.

this

thus

thistle

this line matches too much

A non-greedy version, in contrast, is:

```
/th.*?s/
```

> I want to match **the words that s**tart
>
> wi**th 'th' and end with 's'.**
>
> **this**
>
> **thus**
>
> **this**tle
>
> **this** line matches too much

Earlier in the tutorial, the problems of matching too much were discussed, and some workarounds were suggested. Some regular expression tools are nice enough to make this easier by providing optional non-greedy quantifiers. These quantifiers grab as little as possible while still matching whatever comes next in the pattern (instead of as much as possible).

Non-greedy quantifiers have the same syntax as regular greedy ones, except with the quantifier followed by a question mark. For example, a non-greedy pattern might look like: /A[A-Z]*?B/. In English, this means "match an A, followed by only as many capital letters as are needed to find a B."

One little thing to look out for is the fact that the pattern /[A-Z]*?./ will always match zero capital letters. If you use non-greedy quantifiers, watch out for matching too little, which is a symmetric danger.

Atomic grouping and possessive quantifiers

In Python 3.11, the standard library re module gained features called "atomic grouping" and "possessive quantifiers." The third-party regex Python module had these previously. As well, Python had been somewhat behind Java, PCRE, .NET, Perl, Boost, and Ruby in this regard. Both of these features have the general purpose of avoiding backtracking once a partial match is established (which can both be faster and convey intention better in some cases).

```
/0*\d{3,}/
```

> Integers greater than **100** (leading zeros permitted)
>
> 55 **00123 1234 0001 099 200**

```
/0*+\d{3,}/
```

> Integers greater than **100** (leading zeros permitted)
>
> 55 **00123 1234** 0001 099 **200**

Since both 0 and \d can match the same character, the two quantified patterns get into a contest to grab the longest substring, using backtracking. This gives the wrong answer without the possessive quantifier *+. The quantifiers '++', ?+, and {n,m}+ have analogous meanings derived from their base quantifiers.

```
(?>0*)\d{3,}
```

> Integers greater than **100** (leading zeros permitted)
>
> 55 **00123 1234** 0001 099 **200**

Atomic grouping is a more general version of possessive quantifiers. It also "matches once then stops" to avoid backtracking. However, the pattern within an atomic group—as with a normal group, a lookahead assertion, or a non-backreference group—can be arbitrarily complex rather than governed by a single quantifier.

Pattern-match modifiers

`/M.*[ise]\b/`

> **MAINE # Massachusetts** # Colorado #
>
> mississippi # **Missouri** # Minnesota #

`/M.*[ise] /i`

> **MAINE # Massachusetts** # Colorado #
>
> **mississippi # Missouri** # Minnesota #

We already saw one pattern-match modifier in the modification examples: the global modifier. In fact, in many regular expression tools, we should have been using the g modifier for all our pattern matches. Without the g, many tools will match only the first occurrence of a pattern on a line in the target. So this is a useful modifier (but not one you necessarily want to use always). Let us look at some others.

As a little mnemonic, it is nice to remember the word "gismo" (it even seems somehow appropriate). The most frequent modifiers are:

- g - Match globally
- i - Case-insensitive match
- s - Treat string as single line
- m - Treat string as multiple lines
- o - Only compile pattern once

The o option is an implementation optimization, and not really a regular expression issue (but it helps the mnemonic). The single-line option allows the wildcard to match a newline character (it will not otherwise). The multiple-line option causes ^ and $ to match the begin and end of each line in the target, not just the begin/end of the target as a whole (with sed or grep this is the default). The insensitive option ignores differences between the case of letters.

Changing backreference behavior

```
s/([A-Z])(?:-[a-z]{3}-)([0-9]*)/\1\2/g
```

< A-xyz-37 # B:abcd:142 # C-wxy-66 # D-qrs-93

> **A37** # B:abcd:42 # **C66** # **D93**

Backreferencing in replacement patterns is very powerful; but what do we do if we have a complex regular expression where we need more than nine groups? Quite apart from using up the available backreference names, it is often more legible to refer to the parts of a replacement pattern in sequential order. To handle this issue, some regular expression tools allow "grouping without backreferencing."

A group that should not also be treated as a backreference has a question-mark colon at the beginning of the group, as in `(?:pattern)`. In fact, you can use this syntax even when your backreferences are in the search pattern itself.

Naming backreferences

```
import re
txt = "A-xyz-37 # B:abcd:142 # C-wxy-66 # D-qrs-93"
print(
    re.sub("(?P<prefix>[A-Z])(-[a-z]{3}-)(?P<id>[0-9]*)",
        "\g<prefix>\g<id>", txt)
)
```

A37 # B:abcd:42 # **C66** # **D93**

The Python language (and some others) offers a particularly handy syntax for really complex pattern backreferences. Rather than just play with the numbering of matched groups, you can give them a name.

The syntax of using regular expressions in Python is a standard programming language function/method style of call, rather than Perl- or `sed`-style slash delimiters. Check your own tool to see if it supports this facility.

Lookahead assertions

```
s/([A-Z]-)(?=[a-z]{3})([a-z0-9]*)/\2\1/g
```

> < A-xyz37 # B-ab6142 # C-Wxy66 # D-qrs93 ← **The line has trailing space**
>   **not visible as printed**
> > **xyz37A-** # B-ab6142 # C-Wxy66 # **qrs93D-**

```
s/([A-Z]-)(?![a-z]{3})([a-z0-9]*)/\2\1/g
```

> < A-xyz37 # B-ab6142 # C-Wxy66 # D-qrs93
>
> > A-xyz37 # **ab6142B-** # Wxy66C- # D-qrs93

Another trick of advanced regular expression tools is "lookahead assertions." These are similar to regular grouped subexpressions, except they do not actually grab what they match. There are two advantages to using lookahead assertions. On the one hand, a lookahead assertion can function in a similar way to a group that is not backreferenced; that is, you can match something without counting it in backreferences. More significantly, however, a lookahead assertion can specify that the next chunk of a pattern has a certain form, but let a different subexpression actually grab it (usually for purposes of backreferencing that other subexpression).

There are two kinds of lookahead assertions: positive and negative. As you would expect, a positive assertion specifies that something does come next, and a negative one specifies that something does not come next. Emphasizing their connection with non-backreferenced groups, the syntax for lookahead assertions is similar: (?=pattern) for positive assertions, and (?!pattern) for negative assertions.

Lookbehind assertions

```
/(?<=[AC])-[A-Za-z]+\d+/
```

A-**xyz37** # B-ab6142 # C-**Wxy66** # D-qrs93

```
/(?<![AC])-[A-Za-z]+\d+/
```

A-xyz37 # B-**ab6142** # C-Wxy66 # D-**qrs93**

Similarly to lookahead, we can look *behind* to indicate that a pattern must be preceded by a pattern but not include that prefix in the match. Lookbehind assertions are often limited to fixed width patterns for implementation reasons.

As with lookahead, lookbehind assertions might be either positive or negative. So in our string that might be part numbers, we first want to highlight only those that lead with an A or C, then exclude those that lead with an A or C. Notice that the leading letter, even if it is B or D is not part of what we match.

The example does not do so, but we might exclude the leading hyphen in the matches by using groups and backreferences.

Making regular expressions more readable

```
/                     # identify URLs within a text file
     (?<![="])        # do not match URLs in IMG tags like:
                      # <img src="http://mysite.com/mypic.png">
(http|ftp|gopher)     # make sure we find a resource type
         :\/\/        # ...followed by colon-slash-slash
      [^ \n\r]+       # stuff other than space, newline, tab
    (?=[\s\.,])       # followed by whitespace, period, comma
/
```

The URL for my site is: **http://mysite.com/mydoc.html**. You might also enjoy **ftp://yoursite.com/index.html** for a good place to download files.

In the later examples we have started to see just how complicated regular expressions can get. These examples are not half of it. It is possible to do some almost absurdly difficult-to-understand things with regular expression (but ones that are nonetheless useful).

There are two basic facilities that some of the more advanced regular expression tools use in clarifying expressions. One is allowing regular expressions to continue over multiple lines (by ignoring whitespace like trailing spaces and newlines). The second is allowing comments within regular expressions. Some tools allow you to do one or another of these things alone, but when it gets complicated, do both!

The example given uses Perl's extend modifier to enable commented multi-line regular expressions. Consult the documentation for your own tool for details on how to compose these.

index